100

OUR SENSES GAMES

3 TO 5

Easy-to-play
games

Supporting
early learning

Stages of
development

SU GARNETT

CREDITS

British Library Cataloguing-in-Publication Data A catalogue record for this book is available from the British Library.

ISBN 0 439 97122 5

Author
Su Garnett

Illustrations
Gaynor Berry

Editor
Victoria Lee

Assistant Editor
Jennifer Shiels

Series Designer
Anna Oliwa

Designer
Andrea Lewis

Text © 2004 Su Garnett
© 2004 Scholastic Ltd

Designed using Adobe PageMaker

Published by Scholastic Ltd
Villiers House
Clarendon Avenue
Leamington Spa
Warwickshire CV32 5PR

Visit our website at www.scholastic.co.uk
Printed by Belmont Press

1 2 3 4 5 6 7 8 9 0   4 5 6 7 8 9 0 1 2 3

Acknowledgements

The publishers gratefully acknowledge permission to reproduce the following copyright material:

© **Derek Cooknell:** p5, p6, p7, p8, p9, p10, p11, p15, p16, p17, p18,p28, p29, p32, p33, p34, p39, p40, p47, p49, p50, p51, p52, p53, p54, p55, p57, p64, p65, p67, p69, p70, p71, p72, p73, p74, p80, p84, p85, p88, p96, p97, p98, p104, p107, p110, p111a, p112, p115, p120, p121.

© **Corbis:** Cover.

© **Ingram Publishing:** Cover, p3, p4.

© **SODA:** p97.

© **James Levin/Studio Ten/SODA:** p23.

© **Stockbyte:** p12, p24, p83.

© **Image courtesy of Guide Dogs www.guidedogs.org.uk:** p111b.

Every effort has been made to trace copyright holders and the publishers apologise for any inadvertent omissions.

CONTENTS

CHAPTER 1

CHAPTER 2

CHAPTER 3

CHAPTER 4

CONTENTS

CHAPTER 5

CHAPTER 6

CHAPTER 7

CHAPTER 8

INTRODUCTION

Learning through play

It is important for children to be enthusiastic and to develop an enquiring mind if they are to gain successful learning skills. Everyday situations provide plenty of opportunities for exciting games, which will help to achieve that enthusiasm and curiosity. The 'Our senses' games in this book provide children with the opportunity to be taught in an informal and enjoyable way; they will be learning without realising it!

When children are engaging in imaginary role-play situations, it is relatively easy to appreciate how various skills are being developed. You can hear children practising their language skills as they assume different roles in the setting and talk to one another. You can see them starting to use their emerging writing skills. Children put their physical skills to good use as they dress up and create props for their play, and they increase their social skills by negotiating with others during that play.

This book will show how even the most routine of activities can be turned into an exciting game full of potential for improving learning skills. The games featured in this book have been specifically designed to focus on developing the five different senses – hearing, sight, touch, smell and taste.

The adult's role

In role-play situations, the most effective adult's role is usually a supportive one, only intervening to take action when there seems to be a situation which cannot be resolved any other way. It is, however, often possible to offer simple suggestions for increasing the potential value of the play without a child feeling as if you are taking over, as long as this is done tactfully.

In most of the games in this book, it is necessary for the adult to take on a rather more active role, either by instructing or by helping with some of the more complicated parts of the game. It is also a good idea for the adult to encourage conversation by asking open-ended questions (those to which the answer is not just 'yes' or 'no') and to ask simple questions which encourage children to think 'around' a subject. Children will always learn more in this way as questions stimulate discussion and promote a desire to find out more.

Daily routines and experiences

All the chapters in the book are linked to the everyday routines and experiences of young children. The beginning of a child's day, when he wakes up, gets dressed, has his breakfast and is getting ready for the day ahead is covered in 'Up and About' (Chapter 1). 'Meal times' (Chapter 2), a very important part of any child's day, introduces games which encourage children to use their senses of smell, taste and touch to fully appreciate their food. Children have the chance to use all their senses to the full when they are involved in helping around the home, be it with washing up, cooking, gardening or a number of other activities in 'Helping' (Chapter 3). 'Indoor games' (Chapter 4) concentrates on games which particularly promote children's sense of sight as they play together in the middle of the day. The end of the day, when adults and children share time together before children go to bed is a very special time and 'Together time' (Chapter 5) contains games which concentrate on children's hearing skills.

The last three chapters in the book concentrate on the importance of developing keen senses in 'Outdoor fun' (Chapter 6); how the senses can help children to appreciate other cultures and countries in 'Role-play' (Chapter 7), and the consequences of sense deprivation in 'Friends together' (Chapter 8).

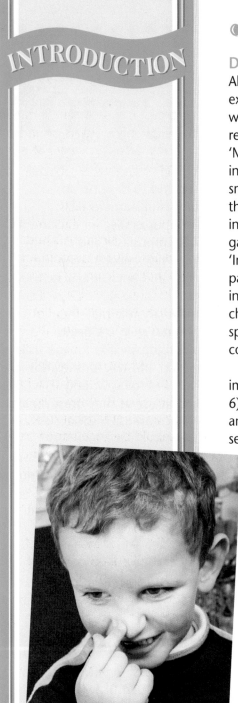

Using their senses

Exploring their senses is a vital learning tool for children as they grow up. As children develop from babyhood, through the toddler stage and on to young childhood, they become more and more aware of their senses and how these can help them in their exploration of the world. Their sense of hearing helps to develop good concentration and a growing vocabulary and, the more this sense develops, the more it will instil in children a love of music, rhymes and stories. As children develop their observation skills, they will become more and more aware of the beautiful things around them. They will be keen to reproduce that beauty in creative work, and will be able to identify similarities and differences, and be aware of change. Using their sense of smell allows them to anticipate the enjoyment of eating different foods, to appreciate flowers and other scents, and to be able to detect potential dangers. Meal times become very much more pleasurable when they are able to identify all the lovely tastes within a meal. They also become acutely aware of hygiene issues (clean or dirty teeth) and illnesses (sore throats) by using their tongues and their sense of taste. Their sense of touch helps them

to explore and understand objects and the environment, and also provides them with much pleasure as they snuggle into warm bedding or stroke a cat's fur.

When children are a little older, they are able to use their senses much more accurately will start to discriminate between many sights, sounds, smells, tastes and textures. Throughout the book, what to expect at each developmental stages is referred to at the beginning of each chapter.

How children learn

Before they are involved with formal schooling, young children will be influenced most by those who look after them – their parents and carers. Those adults have an enormous initial impact on children and will affect the way they learn in the future. Children learn by acquiring a number of different skills. These include developing an enquiring mind, being aware of what is going on around them, gaining the ability to think carefully, to listen, to discuss, to memorise and to concentrate.

Most children are very curious and want to know more, which makes it very easy for adults to encourage this curiosity and channel it to useful effect. Every opportunity should be taken to show children new things and to encourage them to look again at familiar ones, be it at home or when out and about. They should be encouraged to think about how things work, what they are used for and why they react in the way they do. Asking children to think in this way and challenging them to answer their own questions, by observing, exploring, experimenting and discovering, helps them to increase the skills they need to be able to learn effectively. Discussing ideas and thoughts with children is also very important. This helps them to feel valued, more confident and also clarifies issues. The added benefit of developing these various skills is that children will be interested in learning and will feel more motivated to learn in the future. Their enthusiasm for learning will be firmly embedded.

Using the games

All the games in this book concentrate on sensory development. They are designed for use at home or at a childminder's with one or two children, or can easily be adapted for larger groups in a playgroup, crèche, nursery or Reception class. They should be fun. If any game becomes a chore, rather than fun, save the game for another occasion when your child is feeling more receptive. Choose a time when you are both relaxed and can concentrate fully on the point of the game. If playing with more than one child, make sure you allow enough time for each child to have a turn. As you play, you will be showing your child how all the things he normally does in the course of his day can be turned into enjoyable, meaningful, learning experiences. The various opportunities for role-play settings (and the games within these) are particularly useful for promoting discussion and understanding about other cultures and countries. Follow your child's lead and interests, maybe starting with discussion about his holiday to France or his friend who is celebrating Divali.

The activities in the final chapter concentrate on sensory deprivation and these games are designed to help make it easier to tackle this subject with sensitivity. Introduce these particular games slowly, allowing each idea to be fully understood before introducing the next one.

Early learning

Children from the age of three in early years settings – playgroups, nurseries and schools – are taught a curriculum known as the Foundation Stage. The Foundation Stage provides activities and experiences for helping children to make progress in their development and learning. It prepares children for learning in Key Stage 1 of the National Curriculum. It is followed until the end of the Reception year at school when children are approaching six years old. There are six Areas of Learning in the Foundation Stage. These are:

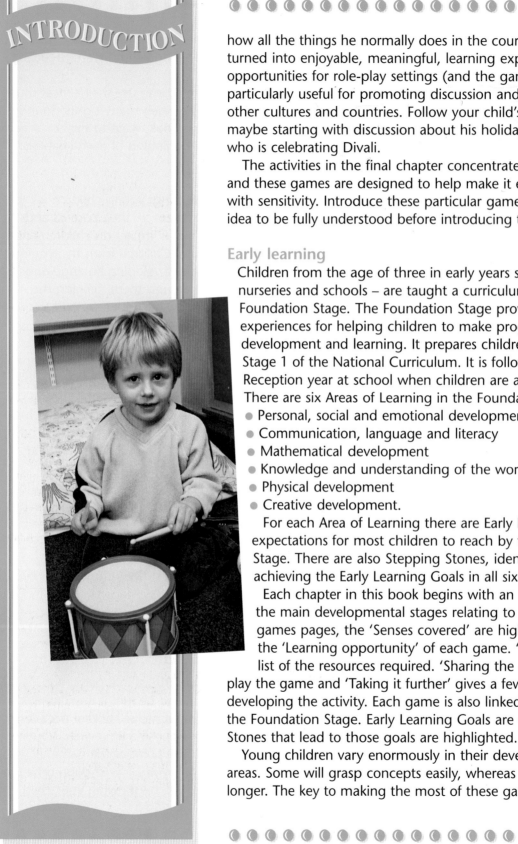

- Personal, social and emotional development
- Communication, language and literacy
- Mathematical development
- Knowledge and understanding of the world
- Physical development
- Creative development.

For each Area of Learning there are Early Learning Goals, which set expectations for most children to reach by the end of the Foundation Stage. There are also Stepping Stones, identifying progress towards achieving the Early Learning Goals in all six Areas of Learning.

Each chapter in this book begins with an introduction, setting out the main developmental stages relating to that chapter. On the games pages, the 'Senses covered' are highlighted before describing the 'Learning opportunity' of each game. 'You will need' sets out a list of the resources required. 'Sharing the game' explains how to play the game and 'Taking it further' gives a few more ideas for developing the activity. Each game is also linked to an Area of Learning of the Foundation Stage. Early Learning Goals are given and the Stepping Stones that lead to those goals are highlighted.

Young children vary enormously in their development in different areas. Some will grasp concepts easily, whereas others will take much longer. The key to making the most of these games is to enjoy them.

UP AND ABOUT

There is nothing more gratifying than feeling a warm, cuddly blanket when you are cold, nothing more satisfying than stroking the smooth, sleek fur on a cat, nothing more glorious than messing around with sticky, gooey finger-paints. In other words, our sense of touch greatly adds to our enjoyment of the world around us and enhances our daily lives. It also helps us to explore and understand new things, and to be reassured by those we love and trust which makes us feel safe.

The games in this chapter focus mainly on the sense of touch, but there are also games involving the other senses as your child prepares for the day ahead.

TOUCH

Our sense of touch greatly increases our enjoyment of the world around us. Whether it is feeling the warmth and comfort of clothing and bedding, the wonderful smooth textures of tiling, the icy feel of snow, the furry feel of some plants or a myriad of other sensations, our sense of touch adds another dimension to our pleasure of all these experiences. All children are keen to explore new things with their hands, and will not need much encouragement to pick things up and feel them. For many three-year-olds, the actual experience of feeling something different will be immensely satisfying. As children grow older, they will want to know how this feeling relates to the other issues surrounding that object, for example, its appearance and its use. Adding the extra information about its texture helps older children to understand more about the object and why it is used in the way it is.

How you can help

● Bearing in mind safety considerations, encourage your child to touch things which are around him at every opportunity.
● Do they feel as he expects them to?
● Invite him to tell you what something will feel like before he touches it. Is the reality the same?
● Help his understanding by making connections between all the various pieces of information from his other senses, for example, feathers are light, they keep birds warm by trapping air in them, they feel fluffy – they are used in duvets to keep us warm.
● What are some of his favourite things to feel? Can he explain why?

SECURITY

Confidence grows slowly with age and experience. A number of three-year-olds can still feel very insecure in new situations and may well still value a 'comforter' (that is, a soft piece of material that they can hold and stroke). It makes them feel in control and safe. Many will also want the reassuring feel of an adult's hand or to be carried in an adult's arms, when they are in unfamiliar environments. As children grow

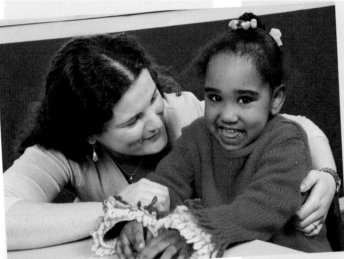

the majority of children will be interested in practising zips, buckles and buttons, and will gradually become more independent in their own dressing. With this independence is likely to come a desire to keep their own hair tidy and to manage other personal hygiene.

older, they become more self-confident, but many still need that reassuring hug when they are upset or hurt. They may also continue to value and love a variety of soft toys.

pointed out to them, they will be capable of noticing the difference between various materials. Most four- to five-year-olds are intensely inquisitive and want to understand exactly why things happen. They will discover that things, which look incredibly similar, can feel very different and behave in very different ways. By using their sense of touch carefully they will be able to discover the answers to many of their questions, such as why some materials are waterproof, why some keep us warm while others are designed to keep us cool, and why certain materials are used for specific things around the house.

How you can help
● Make sure you provide your child with plenty of physical contact in the way of hugs, kisses and a reassuring hand. Lift her into your arms when she wants or needs this, and comfort her with pats or strokes when she is upset.
● Allow her to take a familiar toy or blanket with her when she is going somewhere new or is trying something for the first time.
● Let her have what may seem like babyish toys (soft toys, for example) in her bed as she goes to sleep.

How you can help
● Encourage your child to choose suitable clothing for warm/cold days.
● If he has several suitable outfits, let him express a view about which he would like to wear.
● Try to help your child to become independent in dressing by allowing plenty of time to get ready in the morning and by helping him as little as possible, unless he gets very frustrated.
● Ask your child to help you with your fastenings as well as his own. It is often easier for a child manage these on someone else first.
● Encourage him to brush his own hair and to keep himself tidy.

How you can help
● Encourage your child to notice different materials while explaining how the various properties of those materials make them suitable for particular jobs.
● Point out what happens to different materials in certain situations, for example, what happens when she spills water on the carpet and on a shiny wooden floor?
● Would she independently choose a mac or a warm coat when it is raining hard outside? Why?

Most three-year-olds will attempt to dress themselves and will be generally aware of which clothes are suitable for different weather conditions. Some, however, will still require some help with the various fastenings on clothing and shoes. Between the ages of four and five,

EXPLORING AND UNDERSTANDING
Children learn by using all of their senses to explore objects and the environment. The sense of touch is very important because it helps children to be aware of the different properties of materials. Most three-year-olds are very interested in their surroundings and, if things are

UP AND ABOUT

SENSES COVERED
Hearing.

LEARNING OPPORTUNITY
● To compare mechanical sounds from an alarm clock with the infinite variety of sounds that can be produced by the human voice.

YOU WILL NEED
Variety of alarm clocks.

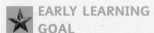

STEPPING STONE
Respond to sound with body movement.

EARLY LEARNING GOAL
Creative development: Recognise and explore how sounds can be changed.

Rise and shine

Sharing the game
● Talk about everyone's need for a good night's sleep and, for younger children, a rest during the day.
● How do we wake up at the correct time?
● Look at the various alarm clocks with your child and explain how they can be programmed to ring at a certain time, so that they wake us up. Listen to the various sounds that they make – bells, bleepers, buzzers. Can the volume of the sound be changed to make them more insistent? Which sound does your child think would wake him up most effectively?
● Many children are actually woken up by their parents and not by an alarm clock. What is your child aware of you saying when you come to wake him up? Does he wake up immediately or do you have to use a louder and more urgent voice to wake him?
● Would he prefer to be woken up by you or a sound from an alarm clock? Why? Discuss the human factors involved.

Taking it further
● Talk about how animals in the farmyard wake up. Listen to a tape of a cock crowing.
● Ask your child to wake you, as you pretend to be asleep. Discuss with him the various tones he used and what effect they had on you.

SENSES COVERED
Touch.

LEARNING OPPORTUNITY
● To identify, enjoy and describe different textures.

YOU WILL NEED
Doll's bedding – duvet, sheet, blanket, mattress and pillow; variety of soft toys.

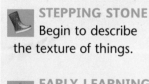

STEPPING STONE
Begin to describe the texture of things.

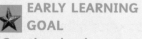

EARLY LEARNING GOAL
Creative development: Explore texture.

Snug as a bug!

Sharing the game
● Discuss the warm, cosy feel of beds.
● Talk about different types of bedding – sheets, blankets and duvets.
● Explain to your child that you are going to ask her to use her sense of touch to choose the most suitable materials for making a comfy bed for one of her soft toys.

● Let your child feel the various types of bedding with her eyes closed. Can she tell which is which, by touch alone? Which would she choose to make a comfy bed?
● Encourage your child to come up with different words to describe the bedding (for example, cuddly, warm, soft, thick) and, also, the reasons for her choice.
● Ask your child to consider how to make the bed comfortable to lie on as well as snug and warm for the soft toy. Invite her to feel the mattress and pillow. Will these make the bed comfortable to lie on? Ask her to describe how the bed would feel if there were no mattress or pillow.
● Look together at the soft toys. Are they all furry? Take it in turns to notice different features. Look out for such things as whiskers that tickle, smooth noses, glassy eyes, rough paws, velvety tummies and so on.

Taking it further
● Ask your child whether her chosen soft toy would always want his bed to feel warm and cosy. Can she think of occasions when the toy would like to feel cool in bed? When it is very hot outside, what bedding would be the most suitable? Can she tell you why?
● Share the rhyme 'I love little pussy' on page 125.

LEARNING OPPORTUNITY
● To be aware of the different textures and different properties of various floor-coverings.

YOU WILL NEED
Different floor-coverings – on the floor and in small samples, for example, carpet, cork tiles, lino, wooden boards and ceramic tiles.

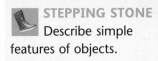

STEPPING STONE
Describe simple features of objects.

EARLY LEARNING GOAL
Knowledge and understanding of the world: Investigate materials by using the sense of touch.

Off to the bathroom!

Sharing the game

● Invite your child to shut his eyes and stand, barefoot, on the floor. Is he standing on soft carpet or hard flooring? How can he tell?

● Ask him to describe the feel of the floor covering as his bare feet touch the floor.

● Lead him, with his eyes still closed, from one room into another. Does the floor-covering change as he moves into the bathroom or toilet? Again, encourage him to tell you how he knows by concentrating on describing the feel of the surface under his bare feet.

● Invite your child to think about the different properties of the floor-coverings in the setting. Which feels warm and which feels cold? Which is rough to the touch and which is smooth?

● Can your child tell you which floor-covering they think will be the slippiest when it is wet? Encourage him to find out by exploring the various floor samples with his hands.

● Let him examine the effect of water on them by sprinkling on a small amount of water and spreading it out. Encourage him to help you wipe up the water afterwards.

Taking it further

● Discuss why different floor-coverings are used for different areas of the house. Which properties are most useful where? Why?

● How will the coverings be kept clean?

SENSES COVERED
Sight.

LEARNING OPPORTUNITY
● To be aware of light and dark, and to notice weather conditions.

YOU WILL NEED
Room which can be made dark with thick curtains; window with a clear view of the sky.

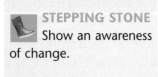
STEPPING STONE
Show an awareness of change.

EARLY LEARNING GOAL
Knowledge and understanding of the world: Look closely at change.

Dark to light

Sharing the game

● When your child wakes in a dark room, point out how little can be seen clearly because of the very limited light. Can she see you clearly enough to identify you, or is she relying on hearing your voice to realise that it is you?

● How do things change when the curtains are drawn?

● It may be still dark outside when your child wakes. If this is the case, opening the curtains obviously has little effect. How can your child make the room light in these circumstances?

● Watch the sky at dawn, as night changes naturally into day.

● Encourage your child to look carefully at the sky and notice the weather conditions, such as blue or grey skies, black clouds and rain, fluffy white clouds and sunshine, leaves blowing in the wind, fog, snow and so on.

● What do these visible signs mean in relation to the weather we can expect during the rest of the day?

Taking it further

● The sun provides bright light in the day and, when it sets, everything goes dark and it is night. On a dank day, when the sky is full of dark grey clouds, ask your child to describe what it is like inside a house in the middle of the day. Can she tell you why it is like that? How can we make it lighter? Talk about electric lighting.

LEARNING OPPORTUNITY
● To be able to tell which clothes are suitable for different weather conditions.

YOU WILL NEED
Selection of clothes in heavy and light materials, such as thick wool, flimsy cotton, quilted, waterproof and furry fabrics.

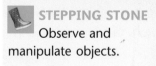

STEPPING STONE
Observe and manipulate objects.

EARLY LEARNING GOAL
Knowledge and understanding of the world: Investigate materials by using the sense of touch.

What shall I wear?

Sharing the game
● Talk about different weathers and the need for different clothes – those which keep us warm, keep us cool and keep us dry.
● Let your child examine the clothes you have assembled, encouraging him to notice the differences between them.
● Can he tell you what makes a particular item of clothing suitable for certain weather conditions?
● Discuss the thickness, weight and texture of the materials.
● Heavy and fluffy materials are good for cold weather, whereas thin, light ones keep us cool. Let your child test out this theory by asking him to wear a thick jersey for a short time in hot weather. He will quickly feel uncomfortable. Equally, he will soon feel very shivery in a flimsy top in very cold weather.
● Can your child tell when a material is waterproof? Show him what happens to rain on a waterproof material by pouring water on to an umbrella or child's mac, and watching the water run off. Compare this to non-waterproof materials where the water soaks through.

Taking it further
● Within reason, let your child select his own clothes to wear in the morning, having looked out of the window and worked out whether he thinks it is hot or cold, and whether he needs something to keep him dry.
● Share the rhyme 'It's raining, it's pouring' on page 125.

STEPPING STONE Respond to simple instructions.

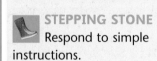 **EARLY LEARNING GOALS**
Communication, language and literacy: Sustain attentive listening, responding to what they have heard by relevant comments, questions or actions.

What's the plan?

Sharing the game

● Start by explaining to your child that most people organise their days so they can manage to fit in everything they want or have to do. At school or nursery, there will be a timetable setting out what is going to happen and when. At home, parents or carers probably will not have a strict timetable, but they will have thought about when they are going to do various things.

● Ask your child to listen carefully as you describe to them a list of what is going to happen today. Divide the day up into meaningful chunks, so that it makes it easier for her to absorb the information (for example, before lunch, after lunch, at teatime and so on).
● If possible, involve your child in the planning by asking what she would like to fit in during the day.
● Make it clear what she is required to do for each stage of the plan. When you have explained the layout of the day to her, see how much she can remember by asking her what her role is during the day for various activities.
● Is she able to respond by appropriate actions?

Taking it further

● Can your child outline your role in the planned day as well as hers?
● Ask your child to plan her own complete morning of activities and games she would like to do.

SENSES COVERED
Touch, sight.

LEARNING OPPORTUNITY
● To understand how various fastenings work.

YOU WILL NEED
Clothing with fastenings of different types, such as buttons, zips, Velcro, buckles; an electric timer.

STEPPING STONE
Examine objects to find out more about them.

EARLY LEARNING GOAL
Knowledge and understanding of the world: Investigate objects and materials by using all of their senses as appropriate.

Do it up!

Sharing the game

● Talk about the most suitable fastenings for different types of clothing and shoes. Encourage your child to look for examples of fastenings among his own clothing.

● Look at buttons and buttonholes. Discuss the appropriate size of buttonholes for different-sized buttons. Why is this important?

● When doing up zips, explain the importance of locking the teeth correctly for the zip to work. Show him how to engage the two sides of an open-ended zip together, before attempting to do it up.

● Ask your child to examine the two surfaces of Velcro by feeling them carefully. One is rough and the other has tiny hooks which grip on to the rough surface of the matching piece.

● Buckles are used mostly on belts and shoes. Point out the series of holes on the strap. Show him how the point of the buckle goes through any of these holes to adjust the tightness of the strap.

● Sew a large button on to an old teddy. Make a suitably-sized buttonhole in a square of strong material. Encourage your child to use both his sense of touch and sight, to practise doing and undoing this button as quickly as he can before the timer pings. Gradually shorten the timer's length as your child becomes more confident.

Taking it further

● When your child is reasonably competent at doing up any of these fastenings, encourage him to try doing up a button or a buckle with his eyes shut, using his sense of touch only.

SENSES COVERED
Touch, sight.

LEARNING OPPORTUNITY
● To learn about keeping hair looking clean and tidy.

YOU WILL NEED
A hand mirror and table mirror; brush or comb.

STEPPING STONE
Demonstrate a sense of pride in own achievement.

EARLY LEARNING GOAL
Personal, social and emotional development: Manage their own personal hygiene.

Beautiful hair

Sharing the game

● Discuss how children's hair varies. Mention colours, length, thickness, curly or straight and so on.

● When we wake up in the morning, our hair is likely to be tousled and in a mess. Encourage your child to feel her hair, without looking in the mirror, when she has just woken up or after she has shaken her head upside down.

● Can she tell that it is in a mess?

● If she pats and strokes her messy hair without using a brush or comb, can she tidy it up?

● Check in the mirror having done this. What does it look like? Does she still need a brush or comb? Can she say why? Is it the same for everyone? Why not?

● In front of the mirror, let her try to brush or comb her tangled hair to make it neat again. Explain why it hurts if she brushes too hard. (All the individual hairs pull at the skin on her head.)

● Talk about combing from the ends of the hair to avoid pulling it.

● How does she know when her hair needs washing? Can she feel that it is greasy?

● Discuss which hair will need more attention – short and straight or long and curly. Why?

Taking it further
● Can your child suggest any ways of keeping unruly hair tidy?

SENSES COVERED
Touch.

LEARNING OPPORTUNITY
● To turn negative feelings into positive ones.

YOU WILL NEED
Your child in bed in the morning; his clothes for the day.

STEPPING STONE
Express feelings in appropriate ways.

EARLY LEARNING GOAL
Personal, social and emotional development: Respond to experiences, showing a range of feelings when appropriate.

I don't want to get up!

Sharing the game
● When your child wakes up in the morning, ask him how he is feeling in his nice, warm bed.
● Ask him to imagine what he will feel like when he gets out of bed.
● Discuss why he might be reluctant to get out of bed. How can he overcome this?
● Talk about how we make ourselves feel warm when we are cold (for example, rubbing hands together, jumping up and down, and putting on warm clothes).
● Discuss what your child will be doing that day.
● When the time has come for your child to get out of bed, see how quickly he can replace his negative feelings with positive ones.
● How does his body feel as he takes off his night-clothes? How does it feel as he starts to get dressed? How does it feel when he is fully dressed? Concentrate on the good feelings that feeling warm again can bring.
● How does your child's mood change when he starts to think about the day ahead?

Taking it further
● Ask him how his body feels when he comes into a warm room after being out in cold or wet weather.
● How does he help his body to feel more comfortable when he gets out of the water after a swim? Talk about large, fluffy towels and warm clothes.
● How does he feel as he has a drink when he is very thirsty or eats a meal when he is hungry?

SENSES COVERED
Sight, touch.

LEARNING OPPORTUNITY
● To be aware of the body's natural reaction to waking up after a sleep and to compare our response with that of a cat.

YOU WILL NEED
Photographs or pictures of cats stretching.

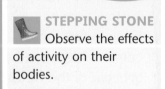

STEPPING STONE
Observe the effects of activity on their bodies.

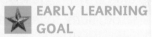

EARLY LEARNING GOAL
Physical development: Recognise the changes that happen to their bodies when they are active.

St...r...e...t...c...h!

Sharing the game

● Look together at the pictures of the cats or, if you own a cat, look carefully at him when he stretches, and notice how he stretches up on his four legs and arches his back high in the air.

● When your child wakes after a sleep, ask her to try stretching like a cat, in order to prepare her body for exercise and activity.

● First, ask her to stand on tiptoe and stretch her legs, so that she is standing as tall as she possibly can.

● Next, ask her to stretch out her arms by raising them high above her body. How tall can she make herself?

● If she stretches her arms out sideways, how wide can she make herself?

● Now, ask your child to kneel on the floor and arch her back up as far as she can, just like a cat would.

● Does she feel any different to usual after this stretching routine?

● When do people stretch? Talk about early morning – getting up after a sleep and stretching helps one to wake up fully. Has she seen you or other members of the family stretching as part of exercise routines? Explain why this is important.

Taking it further

● When your child wakes in the morning, she may still feel very tired. How does her body react? Talk about yawning. This stretches the muscles in her jaw and helps to bring extra air into her lungs, to get her body going.

LEARNING OPPORTUNITY
● To notice the wider environment outside the window.

YOU WILL NEED
A window with a good view.

 STEPPING STONE Show an interest in the world in which they live.

EARLY LEARNING GOAL
Knowledge and understanding of the world: Observe, find out about and identify features in the place they live and the natural world.

What can you see?

Sharing the game

● As your child gets up to start the day, encourage him to look out of his window to see what is happening outside.

● Before you actually look out of the window together, guess what you might be able to see, using your sense of hearing as a clue.

● If it is dark outside, encourage your child to notice various lights. Look out for streetlights, car headlights, lights in houses and so on.

● If it is light, look out for various types of movement, for example, people walking about, cars and lorries driving around, postmen delivering letters, traffic wardens starting work, cows going for milking, tractors going out to the fields, prams being pushed, aeroplanes, birds and so on.

● Encourage your child to be aware that, although he may have just woken up, there is a world out there which has been 'on the go' for some time.

● Discuss the fact that, when he gets up, some people are just going to bed, after a full day's work. Talk about different 'night' workers – nurses, factory workers, night watchmen and so on.

Taking it further

● When you and your child are looking out of the window, take it in turns to tell each other what you see. Do you and your child see the same things?

● Is there more activity early in the morning or later in the day? Can your child tell you why?

SENSES COVERED
Sight, smell, touch.

LEARNING OPPORTUNITY
● To understand how bread changes when it is toasted.

YOU WILL NEED
Several slices of bread; electric toaster.

THINK FIRST!
Never let your child touch the toaster. Keep her at a safe distance as you carefully supervise this game.

STEPPING STONE
Show an awareness of change.

EARLY LEARNING GOAL
Knowledge and understanding of the world: Look closely at similarities, differences, patterns and change.

Breakfast time!

Sharing the game

● Let your child handle some slices of bread, preferably both brown and white. Encourage her to feel the soft texture of the middle of the slice, with the firmer crust at the edges.

● Invite her to smell the bread and notice the fine or more bubbly texture of different breads.

● Look at the colour. Is it uniform or are there patches or specks of other colours? This will obviously depend on the type of flour which your bread is made from.

● Now toast a piece of bread lightly. When it has cooled down, let your child handle the slice again. How has it altered?

● Encourage her to notice how the colour of the bread has changed and to feel how the texture has altered, from soft and spongy to firm and crispy.

● Ask her if it smells different.

● Toast another slice until it is nearly burnt and, again, when it is cool, let her handle it. What colour is this piece? Does it smell nice? Notice how hard it feels.

Taking it further

● Leave the first slice of toast for an hour or so. Now feel it again. Notice how the toast has gone soggy and almost rubbery.

● When your child smells the toast, how does her body react? Does she feel hungry? Is she longing to eat it? Which slice would she like to eat? Why?

● Let her taste both bread and toast. How does the taste change?

CHAPTER 2

MEAL TIMES

Imagine eating your favourite chocolate – your taste-buds immediately get to work! Everyone enjoys eating delicious food and we have all experienced the frustration of losing our ability to taste when we have a cold. Different people like different tastes, and most of us hold very strong views about the food we like and dislike – and the food we are willing to eat or not eat. As well as giving us pleasure, our sense of taste warns us when not to eat something which does not seem to look or taste right. The games in this chapter focus mainly on the sense of taste, with some covering the other senses as we focus on food and meal times.

TASTE

There are a multitude of new tastes for children to experience and enjoy. Many three-year-olds will have tasted only a few of them, but most will be interested in new food. They may well be influenced by other factors, such as the look, smell and feel of the food, before they accept or reject it without even tasting. As children grow older, they are likely to be more reluctant to try anything new, especially if their diet has been somewhat restricted up to now. Even if it has not, they often become fussy eaters at this stage. They are likely to think that any new food is something they will dislike and they will need encouragement to try it. By the time they reach the age of five, they will probably have developed a very firm view as to which food they like and dislike, and it may well be very difficult for you to sway them away from this.

How you can help
- Offer your child as varied a diet as possible from a very young age.
- Try to eat at least one meal with him in the day, so that he gets used to seeing you cooking, eating and enjoying different foods.
- Let your child help you with shopping and putting away food. Allowing him to help you prepare meals introduces him to a wide variety of different foods.
- Within the acceptable limits of good table manners, let him start to enjoy the smell, look and feel of his food, as well as the taste.
- Do not insist that he must eat everything, but encourage him to try different foods.

● Do not give up on introducing new flavours and tastes until your child has been offered the new food several different times. He may well decide that he actually likes something which at first he rejected.

EXPLORATION

Very young babies enjoy exploring things with their mouths. They are not tasting things as such, but are using their very sensitive mouths to tell them about the objects. As children grow older and begin to eat different foods, their true sense of taste comes into play. This sense of taste will in turn become more developed the older the child is. Initially, it will warn them to wait before eating food that is too hot and will discourage them from eating food that is off. At a later stage, children will be able to tell if they need to add sugar to something which is very sour or add flavourings to food which has little or no taste.

How you can help

● Encourage your child to use her sense of taste keenly. Ask her to tell you about all the different tastes of food she is given to eat. Which does she like most and why?
● Make sure she tastes hot food very carefully, to avoid burning her tongue.
● Let your child watch you while you are cooking. How do you decide whether the food you are preparing will be good to eat? Let her see you taste the food as you cook it, and decide whether you need to add sugar or seasoning to make it taste as you wish.
● Try to include her in the tasting process, making sure that the food has cooled down sufficiently. Does she think that you need to add anything?

ILLNESS

When children have colds, their sense of taste is lost and all food tastes much the same. When they have a sore throat, their throats feel dry – very little saliva is produced and it becomes difficult for them to swallow hard food. Certain illnesses produce a rough feeling on their tongues and their whole mouth feels 'wrong'. The mouth is primarily used for tasting, but the tongue has a dual function – to taste and to feel. It is very sensitive and is capable of discerning the smallest differences in the feel of teeth, gums and the lining of both throat and mouth. Hence, it is a very efficient tool when assessing whether we are ill.

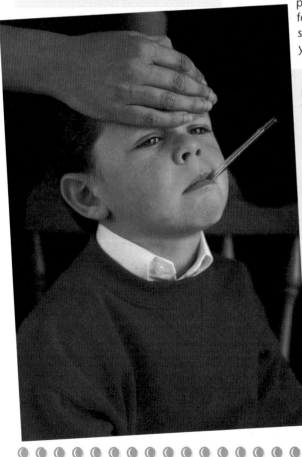

How you can help

● When your child is feeling off-colour, encourage him to describe his symptoms, especially in relation to his senses of taste and touch.
● Encourage him to stick out his tongue and look at it in the mirror. Does it look different to the normal look of his tongue? He may see white patches or tiny spots.
● Ask him to rub his tongue around his mouth. Does if feel different? It may feel quite rough.
● Does food taste different or, indeed, have no taste at all?
● Help him to understand and link his changed and unusual senses with the fact that he is ill.

HYGIENE

When children wake up in the morning, their mouth may feel sticky and their teeth will probably feel rough. The taste in their mouth will probably be rather unpleasant. The routine of cleaning their teeth, either before or after breakfast, cleanses their mouth and makes their teeth all smooth again. The process refreshes their mouth, gives it a pleasant taste and makes it feel more comfortable.

How you can help

● Allow your child to take responsibility for cleaning her own teeth as early as possible. Encourage her by pointing out the pleasant results of clean teeth.
● Make sure she cleans them thoroughly, brushing both the front and back of her teeth, and also gently brushing the gums, especially where the teeth meet the gums.

LEARNING OPPORTUNITY
● To be able to categorise foods into sweet and savoury tastes.

YOU WILL NEED
Several examples of both sweet and savoury food, such as chocolate, sugar, biscuits, cake, raisins, fruit, cheese, ham, vegetables, chicken and pasta dishes.

STEPPING STONE
Show curiosity and interest by facial expression.

EARLY LEARNING GOAL
Knowledge and understanding of the world: Investigate objects and materials by using all of their senses as appropriate.

Sweet and sour

Sharing the game
● Talk to your child about the general make-up of a typical meal. This will usually include some sweet and some savoury items. Sweet items contain sugar and many savoury items contain salt.
● Normally, the meal will begin with savouries, to be followed by a sweet dish.
● Choose two items of food – one savoury and one sweet – and invite your child to remind himself of these tastes by eating a small amount of each.
● Now, show your child all the food you have collected together, and see whether he can sort them into sweet and savoury items just by looking at them.
● Next, allow him to taste the different foods, one by one, to see whether his predictions were actually correct.

Taking it further
● Observe your child as he tastes the various foods. How does his expression vary as he tastes different things? Give him a hand mirror and let him watch his face change as he tastes both food he likes and food that he is less keen on.
● For a very clear reaction to sweet and sour tastes, ask him to taste a very small amount of salt, lemon juice or vinegar, followed by a teaspoon of honey.

SENSES COVERED
Taste.

LEARNING OPPORTUNITY
● To realise that the appeal of some foods is greatly enhanced by being at the right temperature.

YOU WILL NEED
Ice-cream; jelly cubes; chocolate bar; potato.

 **STEPPING STONE**
Show an awareness of change.

EARLY LEARNING GOAL
Knowledge and understanding of the world: Look closely at change.

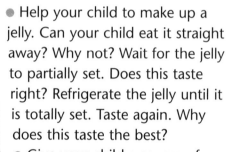

Hot or cold?

Sharing the game
● Remind your child of the story of 'Goldilocks and the Three Bears' (Traditional). Some of the food was too hot, some too cold and some, just right.
● Your child is going to pretend to be Goldilocks and taste some food for you.
● Give your child a bowl of ice-cream. Encourage her to eat some while it is still cold. Does this taste right? Now ask her to leave the rest of it for ten minutes, so that it has totally melted. Taste again. Is this as good or refreshing? Why not?

● Help your child to make up a jelly. Can your child eat it straight away? Why not? Wait for the jelly to partially set. Does this taste right? Refrigerate the jelly until it is totally set. Taste again. Why does this taste the best?
● Give your child a square of a chocolate bar that has been in the fridge. Now, leave the bar out in a warm room until it is beginning to melt. Taste again. Which square was nicer? Why?
● Bake a potato and let your child have some while it is still warm. Let the potato go totally cold. Taste again. Is it still as appetising to her?

Taking it further
● When you are having a hot meal together, let your child see that you keep the food warm in the oven, for second helpings, while you are eating.
● Encourage your child to help you put ice-cream back in the freezer once you have served everyone, to prevent it from melting.
● Share the rhyme 'Pease porridge hot' on page 125.

MEAL TIMES

SENSES COVERED
Smell.

LEARNING OPPORTUNITY
● To understand how our bodies react to the prospect of food.

YOU WILL NEED
Cooking utensils; some favourite food with a strong smell to cook (such as fish fingers, cooking apples, bacon).

STEPPING STONE
Show awareness of own needs with regard to eating.

EARLY LEARNING GOAL
Physical development: Recognise the importance of keeping healthy and those things which contribute to this.

Mmmmm...!

Sharing the game

● Discuss the importance of eating frequently and sensibly, in order to keep healthy.
● Talk about being hungry and the feelings involved.
● Explain that when your child is hungry and he smells food, his mouth starts to produce a liquid called saliva. When your child puts food into his mouth and begins to chew it, this saliva mixes with the chewed food, helping it to be swallowed easily before it is digested in his stomach.

● Can your child tell you what he feels when he is about to eat some food when he is really hungry? (His feelings might include relief, pleasure, excitement and so on.) If he has a pet, encourage him to think about how the pet reacts when he is about to be fed, perhaps by meowing, barking or jumping up and down.
● Just before a meal time, start cooking some strong-smelling food without showing your child what it is that you are cooking. As the smell develops, encourage him to notice the changes taking place in his mouth. Can he tell you what is cooking by smell alone? What does he feel like doing?

Taking it further

● Consider other favourite foods with a strong smell. Which foods make your child's mouth water the most when he smells them?
● Which foods make him most likely to articulate pleasure?

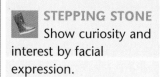
SENSES COVERED
Taste.

LEARNING OPPORTUNITY
● To develop a keen sense of taste.

YOU WILL NEED
Blindfold; pairs of small samples of similar foods with roughly the same texture, but different tastes, for example, pear and apple, cheese-flavoured and plain crisps, peas and baked beans, yoghurt and custard.

 STEPPING STONE
Show curiosity and interest by facial expression.

EARLY LEARNING GOAL
Knowledge and understanding of the world: Investigate objects by using all of their senses as appropriate.

What can I taste?

Sharing the game

● Remind your child about sweet and savoury tastes. It is relatively easy to distinguish between sweet and savoury, but some sweet tastes are very similar and, equally, so are some savoury tastes.

● Explain that you are going to play a game where your child has to try to distinguish between two foods. You will tell her what those two

foods are before she tastes each one in turn and sees whether she can tell you which is which.

● Help your child to put on the blindfold or, alternatively, ask her to close her eyes. Offer her the pairs of food samples in turn.

● Encourage her to taste each sample carefully and really think about the taste before she tells you what she thinks it is.

● If she is not sure of the taste, encourage her to try the other food in the pair and see if she can identify that one. Then invite her to try the first taste again to confirm that it really does taste like the other food in the sample pair.

● Is she better at distinguishing sweet tastes or savoury tastes?

Taking it further

● Offer your child pairs of food samples without telling her what the food is in each pair. Can your child tell you what the samples are?

● Share the rhyme 'Jack Sprat' on page 126.

SENSES COVERED
Taste.

LEARNING OPPORTUNITY
● To learn about the importance of eating well.

YOU WILL NEED
Milk; lunch box; teddy.

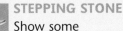

STEPPING STONE Show some understanding that good practices with regard to eating can contribute to good health.

EARLY LEARNING GOAL
Physical development: Recognise the importance of keeping healthy and those things which contribute to this.

My packed lunch

Sharing the game
● Talk to your child about eating sensibly when he is using lots of energy, growing up and running around.
● Explain that food provides our bodies with all the energy we need each day.
● Tell your child that it is good to eat lots of fruit and vegetables, as these help to stop us getting ill.
● Explain that it is also important to drink lots of liquid, especially when it is hot weather.
● Invite your child to prepare a suitable lunch box for one of his teddies.
● Help him to make some sandwiches. Would your child choose brown or white bread, and what savoury filling would he use? Can he tell you why?
● Let him choose fruit or vegetables, or both, and a small amount of energy-giving sweet food.
● What drink would he like to choose?
● Have a picnic. Invite your child to sample the food in his teddy's lunch box. How does it taste? Does teddy like it? Which are your child's favourite tastes?

Taking it further
● Make sure your child understands the importance of eating at least some of all the food in his lunch box, to make sure that he has both foods which give him energy and keep him healthy.
● Can your child think of alternatives foods to bread (for example, sausages or pasta), which would fill up his teddy and give him energy, if he does not like sandwiches?

LEARNING OPPORTUNITY
● To appreciate the difference between a snack and a well-balanced meal.

YOU WILL NEED
Illustrated food magazines for cutting up; scissors; large sheet of sugar paper; felt-tipped pens; PVA glue; empty food packaging, such as biscuit wrappers, crisp packets, Cellophane bags, sleeves from microwaveable meals and so on.

 STEPPING STONE
Sort objects by one function.

EARLY LEARNING GOAL
Knowledge and understanding of the world: Look closely at similarities and differences.

How hungry are you?

Sharing the game

● Discuss with your child what the difference is between a main meal and a snack.
● Invite your child to look through the food magazines and choose a selection of pictures of food to cut out.
● As she does so, encourage her to be aware of the signals her body is sending her. Can she 'taste' or 'smell' the food as she looks at the pictures?
● Draw two large circles on the piece of paper.

● Ask your child to sort the food into that which is suitable for a snack and that which would provide a main meal. Invite her to stick the pictures inside the relevant circles.
● Encourage her to think what it is that makes certain food suitable for snacks. Think about easy packaging and small quantities.
● Invite your child to help you make a display of the empty packaging to show clearly which food is suitable for main meals and which is more for snacks. As she handles the packaging, she may well be able to smell the food that was in it. Is she aware of the taste as well?

Taking it further

● Ask your child to look carefully at the type of packaging used for snacks. This may well include foil, paper, plastic and Cellophane. Let her feel the packaging and identify the different types in this way as well. Which does your child find easiest to open?

MEAL TIMES

SENSES COVERED
Taste, smell.

LEARNING OPPORTUNITY
● To express a preference when offered a choice.

YOU WILL NEED
Bun tins; paper cases for little cakes; a simple cake recipe and ingredients; chocolate, coffee, lemon, orange and strawberry jam flavourings; five plates; felt-tipped pen.

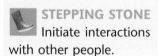
THINK FIRST! Point out the dangers of hot ovens and utensils when cooking.

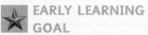
STEPPING STONE Initiate interactions with other people.

EARLY LEARNING GOAL
Personal, social and emotional development: Have a developing awareness of their own views and be sensitive to the views of others.

Happy birthday!

Sharing the game

● Explain that your child is going to pretend to run a shop where customers can come and taste small cakes before they decide what flavour to buy for a big birthday cake.

● His shop provides sample cakes in a variety of flavours for customers to taste.

● He is going to help you to make the sample cakes for the shop in the different flavours.

● Make up a basic cake mix together and then divide the mix into five portions.

● Allow your child to mix some of the flavouring into each portion, before spooning the mixture into the paper cases, putting them in the bun tins and baking.

● Wonderful smells should develop as the cakes are cooking.

● Let the cakes cool before putting on separate, labelled plates ready for the customers to taste.

● Pretend to be one of your child's customers and explain that you have a friend's birthday coming up and that you want to make sure that you choose the right cake.

● Ask your child to tell you what varieties he has on offer and then taste the cakes you choose, before making your final decision.

● Reverse roles and let your child do the tasting.

Taking it further

● Extend the element of choice by offering 'mix and match' icing on the cakes. The flavours could be the same, but you could ask your child to tell you which icing he would like with which cake.

SENSES COVERED
Sight, taste.

LEARNING OPPORTUNITY
● To develop a keener sense of taste.

YOU WILL NEED
Small amounts of green and black grapes; red and green apples; brown and white bread; plates.

STEPPING STONE
Explore objects.

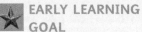

EARLY LEARNING GOAL
Knowledge and understanding of the world: Look closely at similarities and differences.

The same or different?

Sharing the game
● Slice the apples and remove the pips from the grapes, if they have any. Cut the brown and white bread into small cubes.
● Set the food out on to separate plates and show your child the food in pairs (for example, the plates with the green and black grapes).
● First, ask your child to look carefully at the similarities of each pair of foods. Do they look the same?
● Then, encourage her to notice what is different, for example, the skin colour of the fruit or the colour and texture of the bread.
● Next, ask her to taste samples from the two plates in turn. Do they taste the same? At first, they may well taste very much the same to your child, so it might be necessary to encourage her to notice subtle differences by asking relevant questions, for example, 'Are they both as sweet?' or, 'Does one have more flavour than the other?'.

● It is important that your child can express a view as to which she likes best, so finish the game by asking her to eat her preferred samples of food.

Taking it further
● Give your child a piece of milk chocolate and a piece of plain chocolate. Again, examine the obvious similarities, notice differences in the look of the food and then taste for differences. Which does she prefer and why?
● Do the same with cubes of mild and strong cheddar cheese.

Is it ripe?

Sharing the game

● Discuss how bananas grow on tall trees in very hot countries. At first, the bananas are small and green. They gradually increase in size and change colour from green to yellow as the fruit gets softer and sweeter, ready for eating. This is called ripening.

● The green fruit is unripe and the yellow is ripe. When the bananas turn black, they have ripened too much.

● Look at the three bananas together. Do they all feel and smell exactly the same?

● Can your child tell you which fruit is perfectly ready to eat, just by looking at the skins? What about the other two?

● Peel them all without your child seeing and present him with the three peeled fruits. Invite him to guess which is which, having looked, touched and smelled the fruit again.

● Match them up with their original skins.

● Ask him to describe each fruit, using his three senses of sight, touch and smell (for example, the unripe fruit has a greenish skin, is firm with white fruit inside and has very little smell).

● Now, ask him to taste all three fruits. Which does he prefer? Can he tell you why he does not like the other two as much?

Taking it further

● When you go shopping, let your child help you to choose ripe fruit. Point out suitable fruit to buy, concentrating on the skin colour, sweet smell and soft touch.

LEARNING OPPORTUNITY
● To express a preference for still or fizzy drinks.

YOU WILL NEED
Blindfold; still and sparkling mineral water; concentrated cordials; plastic beakers.

STEPPING STONE
Show curiosity, observe and manipulate objects.

EARLY LEARNING GOAL
Knowledge and understanding of the world: Investigate objects and materials by using all of their senses as appropriate.

Fizzy or still?

Sharing the game

● Discuss the importance of drinking plenty in order to keep healthy.
● Many fruit drinks come in both fizzy and still varieties. Ask your child to tell you about any drinks that she particularly likes. Can she tell you whether they are fizzy or still, or is she just talking about the flavours?

● Explain that you are going to make up two drinks in her favourite flavour, one fizzy and one still. You will ask her to put on a blindfold (or close her eyes) and taste each one, before telling you which is which. How can she tell?
● Ask her to describe each one. Which does she prefer?
● Take off the blindfold. Can she tell you which is which, just by looking?
● Leave both drinks for an hour or so. Let your child try them both again. Has anything changed? Can she still tell you which is which? Why not? Explain that the fizzy drinks have bubbles put into them, which disappear into the air after a while, making both drinks taste much the same.

Taking it further

● Let your child listen as you open a new bottle of fizzy drink and one that has been left half-empty for quite a while. Point out the very loud noise of the air escaping from the new bottle and the much quieter sound of much less air escaping from the older bottle. Explain that all fizzy drinks gradually lose their fizz (the tiny bubbles) over time. Compare the sound to opening a bottle of still water.

SENSES COVERED
Taste, sight, touch.

LEARNING OPPORTUNITY
● To understand the difference between fresh and dried fruit.

YOU WILL NEED
Examples of fresh and dried fruit, such as, white grapes and sultanas, black grapes and raisins, plums and prunes, fresh and dried apricots; paper plates.

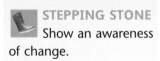

STEPPING STONE
Show an awareness of change.

EARLY LEARNING GOAL
Knowledge and understanding of the world: Look closely at similarities, differences and change.

Fresh or dried?

Sharing the game
● Discuss how lots of fruit can be eaten both fresh and dried.
● Explain that your child is going to play a game where he has to match up the fresh fruit with the dried variety and notice the differences in appearance, texture and taste between the two.
● Put out samples of fruit, not in pairs.
● Encourage your child to use all his senses to examine the fruit.
● Look at the samples first. What is the main difference between the fresh and dried varieties? Look for changes in size, colour and texture.

● Explain that fresh fruit contains lots of water. As it is dried, this water disappears, making the dried fruit much smaller. The colour is also likely to get darker and the texture will be much more wrinkled.
● Now encourage your child to touch the fruit. He should be able to feel that the fresh fruit is smooth, whereas the dried fruit is rough. The dried fruit may also feel sticky.
● Now invite him to match up the various pairs, reminding him of the changes he is likely to find.
● Finally, allow him to taste the fruit pairs, noticing the much stronger and sweeter taste, and the much chewier texture of the dried fruit.

Taking it further
● Explain how dried fruit is very often used in cooking. Sometimes it is necessary to soak the dried fruit in water. Show him what happens to the dried fruit when this is done.

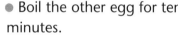

MEAL TIMES

SENSES COVERED
Sight, smell, touch.

LEARNING OPPORTUNITY

● To understand how food changes when it is cooked.

YOU WILL NEED
Two cooking apples; two eggs; two potatoes; cooking utensils.

THINK FIRST!
Point out the dangers of hot rings and utensils when cooking.

STEPPING STONE
Show an awareness of change.

EARLY LEARNING GOAL
Knowledge and understanding of the world: Look closely at change.

Raw or cooked?

Sharing the game

● Explain that you are going to play a game where your child has to guess what will happen to the look, smell and feel of food it has been cooked.

● Let her examine the apple before it is cooked, noting the green skin, sharp smell and hard feel.

● Core the apple and score the skin around the middle. Put it on a baking tray with a little water and cook it in a moderate oven for approximately 45 minutes.

● When the apple is cooked, note the wrinkled, brown skin and soft, white flesh inside, and perhaps an even stronger smell.

● Next, let her crack the egg into a small bowl, noting the lack of smell, the runny texture, the yellow yolk and the clear liquid of the egg white.

● Boil the other egg for ten minutes.

● Point out how the hard-boiled egg smells strongly when removed from its shell and has turned completely firm. The yolk is still yellow, but will probably have a greyish rim around the edge and the egg white has turned white.

● Examine the raw potato, noting the brown or red skin and the hard feel.

● Now peel, cut up and boil the potatoes for approximately 20 minutes in a saucepan. Drain and mash. The potato is now soft, white and fluffy.

Taking it further

● Taste the cooked apple and mashed potato once sugar or seasoning has been added. Would the raw food taste like this? Why not?

MEAL TIMES

SENSES COVERED
Sight, taste.

LEARNING OPPORTUNITY
● To understand some of the needs of small babies.

YOU WILL NEED
Food, such as carrots, parsnips, sweet potatoes and potatoes; sieve; wooden spoon; jars of puréed baby food.

THINK FIRST!
Point out the dangers of hot rings and utensils when cooking.

STEPPING STONE
Show awareness of own needs with regard to eating.

★ EARLY LEARNING GOAL
Physical development: Recognise the importance of keeping healthy and those things which contribute to this.

Food for all

Sharing the game
● Discuss the role of teeth when chewing food.
● Explain that very young babies do not have any teeth. As a result, they need to be given food which is totally smooth. Once they begin to get teeth, they can cope with food that is more lumpy.
● Let your child examine the jars of baby food.
● Ask your child to think about how he could change his food to make it suitable for a tiny baby.
● Peel and chop all of the vegetables, and boil them for about 20 minutes until they are totally soft. Let them cool down.
● Could your child eat the vegetables as they are now? Why?
● Can your child suggest a way to make the vegetables smooth enough for a tiny baby to eat? Encourage him to push a few through the sieve with a wooden spoon and note the very smooth results.

● Compare the taste of the soft-cooked vegetables with the sieved vegetables. Do they taste the same?

Taking it further
● Sieving food is effective in making it smooth, but it is very slow. Let your child see the results of liquidising or food-processing a larger quantity of cooked vegetables. Make sure that he realises that this method is for adults only, as the blades in the machine are very sharp.

LEARNING OPPORTUNITY
● To understand the need for making food look appetising.

YOU WILL NEED
Illustrated cookery books; modelling clay in a variety of colours; paper plates.

STEPPING STONE
Show awareness of own needs with regard to eating.

EARLY LEARNING GOAL
Physical development: Recognise the importance of keeping healthy and those things which contribute to this.

Appetising?

Sharing the game

● Look together at the illustrations of main meals. Ask your child to choose those she particularly likes the look of. Can she tell you why she is drawn to these particular dishes? Notice the contrasting colours of each item of food.

● Help your child to make up various items of food with the modelling clay, that would constitute part of a main meal, for example, brown meat, orange fish fingers, white chicken, white fish, green cabbage, white potatoes, red peppers, green courgettes, orange carrots, yellow cheese, brown gravy and so on.

● Encourage her to mix and match three ingredients for a meal, making up a variety of plates.

● Which meal looks most appetising? Why?

● Help your child to see that a meal made up of ingredients of only one colour will look boring, one made up of only white ingredients will look rather anaemic, whereas one made up of a variety of colours will look exciting and invite the person to want to eat it.

Taking it further

● The texture of foods offered for a main meal also needs to be varied. 'Dry' foods often need to be accompanied by 'wet' ones to make them palatable. Invite your child to try some boiled rice on its own and some with a sauce. Which does she prefer and why?

● Encourage your child to have fun colouring food the 'wrong' colour, using different food colourings, for example, blue mashed potato or green fish. Does this affect the taste or the way your child feels about the food?

CHAPTER 3

HELPING

Imagine a world without any smells. No smoky bonfires to enjoy on 5 November, no waking up in the morning to the smell of bacon and eggs cooking, no beautiful flower scents to appreciate in the spring, not even any perfumes to choose! Not only does our sense of smell greatly enhance our enjoyment of life, but, used together with the other senses, it is an invaluable tool in warning us of things which are not quite right and in helping us to avoid dangers. The games and activities in this chapter suggest a variety of ways in which children can be involved in helping us with everyday tasks. The games concentrate on our sense of smell.

SMELL

Children's sense of smell becomes more acute as they grow older and as they become more aware of the world around them. For many three-year-olds, most smells are likely to be connected with food in one way or another. They will also be very aware of smells to do with bathtime and the comforting smell of close adults. Four-year-olds will probably be more aware of smells outside the home and will start to notice the smell of flowers, grass and different shops. When children reach the age of five, they will be increasingly interested in everything that is happening and will be able to identify specific smells in different environments, together with the smells of various activities going on close by.

How you can help

● Encourage your child to help you in the kitchen when you are putting food shopping away and also when you are preparing and cooking it. Point out the different smells.

● Take him shopping with you and note the different smells in each shop. Look together at what is causing those smells.

● Let him help in the garden. Tell him about the different smells of flowers, grass, leaves and soil, and encourage him to identify all these.

● As you go out and about, point out different smells in the environment, such as cooking smells from cafés and restaurants, petrol fumes in garages and from traffic, bonfires, tarmac where there are roadworks, new paintwork, gas where new pipework is being fitted, smoke from factories and so on.

● Which smells does he find unpleasant and which does he like? Why?

FOOD SMELLS

Familiar food should have a familiar smell. When it does not, it is indicative that something is wrong. Even very young children will be able to smell when food smells completely different, but they

may not be aware of subtle changes and might need to have these pointed out to them. Before food is totally unfit for consumption, it is likely to smell somewhat different and this needs to be recognised if children are to avoid stomach upsets.

How you can help

● Let your child smell the different foods she is helping you to prepare, so that she gets used to the usual smell of various ingredients.

● As you break open eggs or open a new bottle of milk, let her see you smelling the contents to make sure that they smell as they should.

● Point out that smelling your food prior to eating it is not very polite, but it is acceptable to smell it when you are preparing it, to make sure that it is fresh and hasn't gone off.

● Encourage your child to look very carefully at food as well as smelling it to see if it looks any different (very often it will if it is not fresh).

● Ask her to describe the smells of both fresh and 'off' food. Are either of the smells pleasant or unpleasant?

DANGERS

Very strong smells can indicate impending danger. Escaping gas gives off a very unpleasant smell to warn people to leave the area quickly. Fire is also very easily identified by the strong smell. Three-year-olds need to be protected from potentially dangerous situations, as they will not be able to understand these warning signals by themselves. However, as children get older and more aware, they can be helped to recognise smells which spell out danger and, therefore, those which they should quickly avoid.

How you can help

● Tell your child to alert you or another adult when he notices any smell he does not recognise. Many will turn out to be harmless, but some may well indicate something to be wary of and will need him to take immediate action.

● In a situation where it is totally safe for him to do so, let your child smell 'burning' smells, so that he is able to recognise them in the future. The smells might include bonfires, a burning candle or food that is burning in a saucepan.

HYGIENE

Three-year-olds are learning about hygiene and most will be able to wash independently and go to the toilet by themselves. However, there is still likely to be the occasional accident and children will be very aware of this, because of the uncomfortable feel and the unpleasant smell. They will be very conscious of the difference between clean, dry pants and wet, soiled ones. Obviously, the older children

become, the more conscious they will be of the smells associated with toilet accidents and also other bodily odours. They will be increasingly aware of the need for a bath.

How you can help

● Encourage your child to be independent about going to the toilet when she is ready. Make sure she goes as soon as she needs to, rather than waiting and having an accident.

● Make sure your child washes her hands carefully, after going to the toilet.

● Make bathtime fun, so that your child is always eager to have a bath.

● Point out your child's dirty, smelly hands when she has been doing something messy and encourage her to wash carefully.

● Help her to understand the need for keeping clean by showing her the dirty kitchen floor that needs washing or encouraging her to smell the muddy dog (after a long walk) or the hampster's bedding which has not been changed for a few days.

HELPING

LEARNING OPPORTUNITY
● To identify different smells associated with different types of shops.

YOU WILL NEED
Visit to a supermarket; selection of foods and household goods, such as fresh bread, chocolate, real coffee, fresh fish (if possible), soap; selection of strong-smelling fruit and vegetables (apples, oranges, lemons, leeks); blindfold.

 STEPPING STONE Show an interest in what they smell.

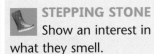 **EARLY LEARNING GOAL**
Creative development: Respond in a variety of ways to what they smell.

Where am I?

Sharing the game

● Talk to your child about supermarkets and how they differ from normal shops. Explain that they are much bigger and that the shop is divided into certain areas or aisles where different types of goods are sold. Many areas can be distinguished by their smell.

● Before you start your shopping, walk your child around the supermarket, talking to him about the smells of various foods and other goods being sold in the different areas.

● Help him to identify the smells associated with each area in the supermarket, for example, the fish counter, the bakery, and the fruit and vegetable section.

● As you go around for the second time, collecting your shopping, ask your child to predict when you are coming near a certain area of the supermarket by identifying the smells coming your way.

● At home, play a game with your child. First, help him to put on the blindfold or, alternatively, ask him to close his eyes. Then, encourage him to smell the items of food and household goods you have collected, in turn, without touching them. Do the smells remind him of the smells in the supermarket? Can he tell you what he is smelling?

Taking it further

● Ask your child if all the smells are pleasant (such as chocolate and coffee). Are some very similar?

● On subsequent visits to the supermarket, encourage your child to enhance his sense of smell by seeing if he can identify different and similar smells, such as fruit and flowers, or soaps and household cleaning items.

SENSES COVERED
Smell, sight.

LEARNING OPPORTUNITY
● To learn how to keep things in order.

YOU WILL NEED
Bags of perishable food, including fruit, vegetables and dairy products.

 STEPPING STONE Examine objects to find out more about them.

EARLY LEARNING GOAL
Knowledge and understanding of the world: Investigate objects and materials by using all of their senses as appropriate.

Nice and fresh!

Sharing the game
● Explain that perishable foods need to be kept carefully and checked regularly, to make sure they have not gone off.
● Let your child feel some of the food that is in your fridge to see how cool it is. Explain that the low temperature of the fridge allows perishable food to be kept for much longer.
● Explain that you want your child to help you to put your shopping away in the right place, checking that none of the existing food should be thrown out because it is no longer suitable to eat.
● Start with the fruit and vegetables. Invite your child to check any remaining in your basket. Tell her that she needs to look out for brown patches or greyish mould on skin and peel, wrinkled, browning leaves and skin, and any squashy or nasty smelling fruit and vegetables.
● Ask her to throw away any 'bad' fruit and vegetables.
● Open any old bottles of milk or cartons of cream that are still in the fridge. Let your child check the contents for any unpleasant smells.

Explain that dairy products which need to be thrown away will have a very strong smell and will also look different, because they begin to separate out or solidify.

Taking it further
● Encourage her to sort your other shopping and help you to put it away in the right cupboards.
● Explain about sell-by dates and let your child see you checking these.

SENSES COVERED
Smell, sight.

LEARNING OPPORTUNITY
● To learn a little about cooking food.

YOU WILL NEED
Cocktail sausages; biscuit dough made from 115g softened butter, 225g castor sugar, one egg, one tblsp milk, 170g plain flour, half a tsp baking powder and half a tsp salt; pastry cutters; baking trays; timer; oven gloves.

THINK FIRST!
Wash hands both before and after handling raw food. Take care when examining hot food.

STEPPING STONE
Show an awareness of change.

EARLY LEARNING GOAL
Knowledge and understanding of the world: Look closely at change.

Let's have a party!

Sharing the game
● Let your child help you to arrange the sausages on a baking tray and to prick them, noting both the smell and look of the raw food.
● Work the sugar, egg and milk into the butter. Add the sifted flour, baking powder and salt. Let your child help you to work the mixture into a firm dough, before rolling it out, cutting out shapes and putting these on to a baking tray. Again, encourage him to look very carefully at the raw food and smell it.

● Put the trays in the oven at 375°F/180°C/Gas Mark 5 and discuss how sausages and biscuits look golden when they are cooked. Talk about approximate cooking times.
● Ask your child to guess exactly how long both foods will take to cook and then invite him to check his guess by using his senses of smell and sight. Set the timer for the length of time he suggests.
● When the timer goes off, invite your child to look at and smell the cooking food. Is it done yet? How can he tell? How much longer will it need? Set the timer again if necessary.

Taking it further
● Make some chocolate crispies by melting a bar of chocolate and stirring in some crispies while still warm. Put spoonfuls into paper cases. Note the strong smell of the melted chocolate and how the crispies fall apart when they are warm, but cling together once they have cooled down.

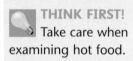

HELPING

LEARNING OPPORTUNITY
● To practise simple subtraction.

YOU WILL NEED
Play dough in both red and white; rolling pins; pastry cutters; bun trays; teaspoon; real pastry; jam.

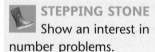

THINK FIRST!
Take care when examining hot food.

STEPPING STONE
Show an interest in number problems.

EARLY LEARNING GOAL
Mathematical development: In practical activities and discussion begin to use the vocabulary involved in adding and subtracting.

The Queen of Hearts

Sharing the game

● Read the rhyme 'The Queen of Hearts' on page 126.
● Encourage your child to roll out the white play dough and to cut out 'pastry' tarts.

● Ask her to cut out smaller circles of red play dough for the 'jam' filling.
● Help your child to assemble the 'tarts' and put them on a plate. Do they smell of anything? How many are there?
● Invite your child to help you roll out real pastry and cut out circles to fit the bun tins. Fill each pastry case with a spoonful of jam.
● Before you cook the tarts, ask your child to smell them. Do they smell different to the pretend ones?

● Next, cook them in the oven at 400°F/200°C/Gas Mark 6 for about ten minutes.
● When they come out of the oven, notice how strongly they smell. Again, make comparisons with the pretend ones. Count how many there are.
● Play a game with the play dough tarts, where your child pretends to be the Knave of Hearts trying to steal the tarts.
● While you close your eyes, she must remove some. You have to count how many are left and, therefore, how many have been taken.
● Reverse roles and help your child to work out how many have been stolen. Return the tarts and see if her answer is the same.

Taking it further

● Pose simple problems for your child to solve, using the actual tarts to help her, for example, the Queen has three real tarts and four pretend ones. How many does she have altogether?

HELPING

SENSES COVERED
Smell, hearing.

LEARNING OPPORTUNITY
● To enjoy preparing for a big celebration.

YOU WILL NEED
Branches of fir; red baubles; tray; oranges; lemons; cinnamon sticks; fresh herbs; knife (for adult use only); baking tray; balloons and pump; rubber bands; string; scissors.

THINK FIRST!
Warn your child not to over-pump balloons.

STEPPING STONE
Talk freely about their home and community.

EARLY LEARNING GOAL
Personal, social and emotional development: Have a developing respect for their own cultures and beliefs and those of other people.

Christmas is coming!

Sharing the game
● Discuss different celebrations and invite your child to help you get ready for Christmas.
● Cut the oranges and lemons into thin slices. Point out the strong citrus smell.
● Bake the slices in a very low oven for at least an hour until firm.
● Let your child tie several cinnamon sticks together with rubber bands and separate out sprigs of herbs, again noticing all of the different smells.
● Invite your child to lay the fir in the tray, noticing the strong smell of the pine needles and let him decorate it with baubles, citrus slices, cinnamon sticks and herbs.
● Show him how to soften the balloons by rubbing them in the palm of his hand.
● Demonstrate how to use the pump and then let him blow up the balloons by himself.
● Help him to slide the balloon off the pump and tie a knot in it.
● Listen to the sound of the air being pumped into the balloons. Hear the hissing sound made if a little air escapes by mistake and also the noise made when the full balloon is let go deliberately.
● Help your child to hang up the balloons in big bunches.

Taking it further
● Play some Christmas music to fully set the scene.
● Heat up some mince pies and enjoy the Christmas smell.

In the garden

Sharing the game

● Explain that you are going to ask your child to plant her own little garden in a corner of your garden or in a deep baking tray.

● Show her the various seed packets you have collected and invite her to choose some flowers she would like to use in her garden, by looking at the different pictures on the packets.

● Encourage her to think about the colours that will come up once the seeds flower. Will they look good together?

● Help her to put a mixture of soil and compost into the tray and mix it together with her hands. Or, she could dig a small area in the garden so the soil is broken up.

● Encourage your child to notice the different feel and texture of the solid blocks of compost and clods of earth, and the dug earth or broken-up compost.

● Help your child to plant the seeds, covering these with more soil and compost, before watering them carefully.

● Compare the feel of dry and damp soil. How will your child know when her plants need watering?

Taking it further

● Make sure your child continues to use her senses of sight and touch to examine the growing seeds and flowering blooms.

● Instead of seeds, let your child plant some small bulbs in the garden or in flower pots, by pushing these well down into the prepared soil or compost.

SENSES COVERED
Smell, sight.

LEARNING OPPORTUNITY
● To learn more about flowers and be creative about displaying them.

YOU WILL NEED
Different coloured flowers; greenery; vases.

THINK FIRST!
Be sure to choose flowers and greenery which are not poisonous and make sure your child washes his hands after handling them.

STEPPING STONE
Choose particular colours to use for a purpose.

EARLY LEARNING GOAL
Creative development: Explore colour, texture, shape, form and space in two or three dimensions.

Beautiful flowers

Sharing the game

● Look at some flowers, together, in turn, identifying some of their characteristics (such as colours, patterns, size, petal shape, overall shape, and type of stem and leaf).

● Does the flower have a distinctive smell? Encourage your child to think about where he might have smelled similar scents before (for example, in flower shops or when handling soaps and other cosmetics in chemist shops).

● Ask your child if he can see any pollen.

● If you have grown any of the flowers, let your child pick his favourite prior to arranging them.

● Allow him to select the flowers he wishes to arrange, paying particular attention to the colours he likes.

● Let your child choose a suitable vase for arranging his flowers. Ask him what size he thinks he will he need.

● Encourage your child to include some greenery and give him help as required (with trimming flowers and greenery), so that the finished arrangement is as your child wishes it to be.

Taking it further

● Instead of a vase, suggest using a basket filled with oasis (floral foam).

● Explain how the oasis works and let your child help to soak it in water prior to use. Ask him which flowers he thinks will have strong enough stems to stick easily into the oasis.

● Look through flower books together, identifying any flowers your child may recognise.

SENSES COVERED
Touch, sight.

LEARNING OPPORTUNITY
● To help with an important everyday task.

YOU WILL NEED
Two plastic bowls; drying rack; washing-up liquid; washing-up brush; plates and cutlery with dried-on food residue.

STEPPING STONE
Show awareness of a range of healthy practices with regard to hygiene.

EARLY LEARNING GOAL
Physical development: Recognise the importance of keeping healthy and those things which contribute to this.

Washing-up time!

Sharing the game
● Collect all the dirty dishes after lunch.

● Fill both bowls with warm water and ask your child to squirt a little washing-up liquid into one, before swirling the water with her hands to create a bubbly solution.

● What is the difference in feel between the ordinary warm water and the soapy water?

● Let your child look carefully at the plates to see where the dirty marks are. Invite her to feel the difference between the rough food residue and the smooth plate. Tell your child that soaking the plates helps to soften the food residue, making it easier to remove.

● After soaking, encourage her to clean the plates with the brush.

● When she is satisfied that these are clean, invite her to rinse them in the second bowl and then to check again that they are totally clean, by looking at them and running her fingers over them.

● Next, do the same with the cutlery. She will need to look even more carefully this time, to make sure that no food residue remains, especially in between the prongs of the forks.

Taking it further
● Let your child try to clean a greasy saucepan with ordinary water and then, again, in soapy water. Ask her if she notices a difference. Explain how the washing-up liquid mixes with the grease to make it easier to remove.

**LEARNING
OPPORTUNITY**
● To enjoy living in a
clean environment.

YOU WILL NEED
Dusters; polish; small
brush and dustpan.

STEPPING STONE
Operate equipment
by means of pushing and
pulling movements.

**EARLY LEARNING
GOAL**
Physical development:
Use a range of small and
large equipment.

Spring-cleaning

Sharing the game

● Tell your child that he is going to be a 'magic robot' who makes
your house all beautifully clean.

● Explain that all surfaces become dusty, and the carpets and floors
collect dirt.

● Point out the dull
look of dusty surfaces.
Encourage your child
to run his hands over
one and notice the
clean marks his fingers
leave on the surface.

● Next, put on the
polish – either a small
amount of cream,
wax or spray. If using
spray, help your child
to point the arrow of
the can in the right
direction, so that the
polish ends up on
the surface and not
on him!

● Encourage your child to make firm, circular movements with his
duster, so that the polish is well worked in. Point out how the surface
changes from being dull to shiny. Notice the clean, fresh smell.

● Sweep a floor, gathering all the dust into one place. Encourage your
child to use the small brush to sweep this dust into the dustpan,
which you hold for him, leaving the floor clean.

● Compare the smell of the dust in the dustpan with that of the
newly-cleaned house.

Taking it further

● How else could your child make the house smell clean and fresh?
Talk about putting a vase of flowers on the table or using air
freshener. Let him smell the results of doing these.

LEARNING OPPORTUNITY
● To realise when clothes need to be washed and how to wash them successfully.

YOU WILL NEED
Assortment of dirty washing; sorting baskets.

 STEPPING STONE
Examine objects to find out more about them.

EARLY LEARNING GOAL
Knowledge and understanding of the world: Investigate objects and materials by using all of their senses as appropriate.

Wash day

Sharing the game
● Ask your child to pretend that she is the owner of a laundry where clothes are washed.
● Explain why she needs to sort the laundry before washing it. Tell her that white clothes can be washed at a higher temperature than coloured ones, and that dye used for colouring dark clothes can leak out of them, so dark colours should always be washed separately to avoid the other washing turning a dark colour.
● Encourage your child to look closely at the washing. Notice where the dirtiest marks are – usually around collars and cuffs, and, on children's clothes, often on the knees and the front of clothes.
● Separate the white clothes first. Then, encourage her to look at the coloured ones and decide which could be washed together and which need to be washed on their own.
● Put the washing in your machine, in several loads if necessary, or wash by hand.
● Let your child help you hang the clothes out to dry.
● When they are completely dry, invite her to sort the clothes again, looking out for clothes that need to be ironed, clothes belonging to different family members, matching pairs of socks and so on.

Taking it further
● Invite your child to sort out her dolls', teddies' and other toys' clothes in the same way.
● If possible, show your child an example of something very dark which has been washed with something white, by mistake. Notice how the resulting item is now a dirty greyish-blue.

LEARNING
OPPORTUNITY
● To learn how to clean
boots and shoes.

YOU WILL NEED
A bowl of water; apron;
sponge; blunt scraper;
shoe polish; shoe
brushes; dusters; muddy
and clean wellington
boots (adult size); pair of
scuffed shoes (adult size);
newspaper.

STEPPING STONE
Engage in activities
requiring hand-eye co-
ordination.

**EARLY LEARNING
GOAL**
Physical development:
Handle tools safely and
with increasing control.

Shoe cleaning

Sharing the game
● Cover the floor with newspaper.
● Examine the clean boots together first, drawing your child's
attention to the ridged patterns on the soles.
● Now look carefully at the muddy boots and notice how the dried
mud has got stuck around the patterns in the soles. Point out the
musty smell.
● Invite your child to use the scraper to remove the mud, holding it
firmly to make sure it does not slip and hurt his hand. He will need to
work the scraper in and around the ridges in the soles to make sure all
the mud falls away. When he thinks he has finished, encourage him to
have a further careful look to make sure that all the mud has gone.
● Next, ask him to clean the surface of the boots using a wet sponge
to rub the mud away. The boots will need to be rinsed carefully to
make sure that no water ends
up inside them.
● With the scuffed shoes, start
by looking carefully to see
whether any dirt can be
scraped off. If not, invite your
child to apply a small amount
of shoe polish to the brush
and brush this carefully over
the entire shoe. Point out the
smell of the polish.
● Once the polish is dry, let
him use the brush or duster
to create a shine. Notice the
clean smell.

Taking it further
● When both boots and
shoes are clean and dry,
compare the different
smells of leather shoes and
rubber wellington boots.

SENSES COVERED
Sight, hearing.

LEARNING OPPORTUNITY
● To learn how to listen carefully and perform a useful task.

YOU WILL NEED
Cutlery; plastic plates and glasses; table mats; some of your child's toys.

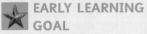
STEPPING STONE
Count out up to six objects from a larger group.

★ **EARLY LEARNING GOAL**
Mathematical development: Say and use number names in order in familiar contexts.

Laying the table

Sharing the game

● Tell your child that she is going to lay the table for a party for some of her toys.

● Discuss how many toys there will be.

● Consider together how many plates and glasses will be needed.

● Talk about what the meal is going to be. Discuss how many plastic knives, forks and spoons she will need, bearing in mind what kind of food requires which type of cutlery.

● Encourage her to listen carefully to what is being said and, therefore, how she responds.

● Having worked out what your child will need, invite her to start laying the table, beginning with the mats. How will she fit them all on to the table? How much space will there be between each one?

● Now invite her to place the cutlery around the mat. As she lays the table, discuss the need for one plate, knife, fork, spoon and glass for one toy.

● What difference will it make if other toys decide to come at the last minute? How many more of everything will she need?

Taking it further

● Bearing in mind the size of your family, can she tell you how many of everything she will need if she lays the table for you? If Grandma and Grandpa are coming to stay, how many more will she need?

The first signs of spring, wonderful clear blue skies, the detail on a bird's feather or a butterfly's wing, and the early morning dewdrops on a spider's web. These are only a few of the delights we can share when we use our eyes to look carefully at the world around us. Our eyes are one of the most useful senses, allowing us not only to enjoy things that we see everyday, but also to search for things or people, to recognise friends, family members and places, and to notice any potential dangers or hazards.

The games in this chapter are familiar activities which have been given a slightly different focus. Nearly all these indoor games concentrate on the sense of sight.

INDOOR GAMES

SIGHT

As with all their senses, children's sense of sight becomes more refined as they grow older. Three- to four-year-old children, when asked to paint a picture, will probably use primary colours and will not be very interested in the shades that can be produced by mixing colours. It is not until children reach the age of five or above that they become intrigued by the full range of possible colours they can produce. Only then will they be able to distinguish a dark from a light green. With regard to detail, young children need to have this pointed out to them. Older children may well be able to show you detail, but neither of these age groups will be able to reproduce much detail in a drawing. That comes later.

How you can help

● Point out to your child all the wonderful colours around him, comparing dark with light and bright with dull.
● Look at pictures together and notice the finer detail.
● Encourage your child to look up at the sky and notice how it changes all the time.
● Encourage him to look out for shadows and the objects that are causing those shadows.
● Ask him to help you find something you have lost by looking carefully in lots of different places.
● Talk about the four seasons and what your child should expect to see at these different times of year.
● Ask him where he is when he reaches a familiar destination. How does he know? What does he recognise?

CREATIVITY

Most children love being creative. They draw, paint and use glue with great enjoyment to produce pictures, cards and models. At the age of three, their efforts will be fairly simple. It may not be very obvious to us what it is they are trying to create, but they will know exactly. Four- to five-year-olds are capable of more detailed work and will often use a variety of media, such as paint, colouring crayons, wool, fabric and other collage materials to create the effect they desire.

How you can help
● Encourage your child to make her own cards and presents to give for birthdays and other celebrations.
● Refrain from asking her what something is. Instead, ask her how she has made it, what she did first and how she chose the colours.
● Treat her creations for what they are – an expression of her enjoyment when using the various media on offer.

GATHERING INFORMATION
Our eyes help us to gather lots of information about the world around us. This lets us understand what is going on. By looking at the sky, we can tell that clouds are blown along by the wind. By looking at a ball being kicked, we can see that round things roll. By looking at trees carefully, we can see that some have green leaves and some have brown. If three-year-olds are encouraged to notice some of these things, they

will hopefully be pointing them out to you when they reach the ages of four and five years old.

How you can help
● Encourage your child to look very carefully at things when you are out and about together. When you notice something unusual or interesting, point it out to him.
● Help him to be aware of some of the less obvious things he is likely to see in different environments, for example, wild flowers in the country or zebra crossings in the town centre.
● When your child shows you something he does not understand, try to answer his questions as clearly and informedly as you can.

SIMILARITIES AND DIFFERENCES
Children learn to distinguish objects and materials by using all their senses, but their sense of sight is very important during their initial investigations. By carefully examining objects, children will be able to tell whether they are the same or different. They will be able to match up patterns and shapes, and recognise things which have changed. Three-year-olds begin to match shapes when completing simple puzzles, putting socks into pairs or finding their matching wellington boots. Four-year-olds can complete more complicated puzzles, should be able to name and match specific shapes in the local environment, and will be able to see both the similarities and the differences in a wide variety of objects.

Most five-year-olds love to help in the kitchen and will be fascinated by how things change as they are mixed

together and then cooked. The majority of them will also enjoy the challenge of looking carefully, and saying whether two similar things really are the same or, on closer inspection, different.

How you can help
● Let your child experiment with puzzles and matching cards, to give her lots of practice in noticing similar shapes, designs and patterns.
● Encourage her to help you put away matching pairs of socks and clothing belonging to different family members.
● Look out for specific shapes, both inside the home and outside. Are these shapes exactly the same or just almost the same?
● Invite your child to help you with simple cooking. Point out how a brown and a white egg look different on the outside, but are the same when they are broken open.
● Point out how the raw cake mixture looks different once it is cooked.

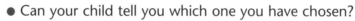

INDOOR GAMES

SENSES COVERED
Sight.

LEARNING OPPORTUNITY
● To identify objects from their description.

YOU WILL NEED
A collection of soft toys and hand puppets.

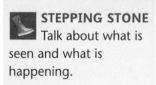
STEPPING STONE
Talk about what is seen and what is happening.

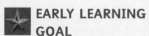
EARLY LEARNING GOAL
Knowledge and understanding of the world: Look closely at similarities, differences, patterns and change.

I spy

Sharing the game

● Spread out the soft toys in a long line so that they are clearly visible to both yourself and your child.

● Ask your child to describe a toy to you, concentrating on colour, size, eye colour, type of fur, number of legs and so on.

● Explain that you will be playing a game where you will ask your child to guess which of the toys you are thinking about, by giving him a brief description of some of its features.

● Proceed as follows, choosing your clues to suit the soft toys in your collection. Restrict the clues to two descriptions at first, for example, 'I spy with my little eye a soft toy which is brown and has tiny blue eyes'.

● Can your child tell you which one you have chosen?

● Make the clues increasingly difficult, so that the answer is not immediately obvious. Your child will have to work through several clues, eliminating possibilities, before reaching the answer. For example, 'I spy with my little eye a soft toy which has very soft fur, but it doesn't have green eyes and it has more than two legs'.

● Take it in turns with your child to pose clues, look very carefully and guess answers.

Taking it further

● If possible, progress on to a collection of smaller toys – finger puppets, small cars, soldiers or something similar.

● The game is essentially the same, but your child will have to look more carefully because the objects are that much smaller.

SENSES COVERED
Sight.

LEARNING OPPORTUNITY
● To enjoy role-playing.

YOU WILL NEED
Dressing-up clothes, including hats, shoes and jewellery if possible; flesh-coloured sugar paper; a large plate; felt-tipped pens; face-paints; hand mirror and long mirror.

STEPPING STONE
Use available resources to create props to support role-play.

EARLY LEARNING GOAL
Creative development: Use their imagination in art and design, imaginative and role-play.

Dressing up

Sharing the game
● Choose a theme, such as 'book characters', and invite your child to dress up in a suitable way to look like her chosen character.
● Encourage her to use the clothing and accessories in an imaginative way, not necessarily using them in the way that is intended, for

example, she might use a long, floaty skirt as a cloak.
● Offer practical help as necessary, but make sure your child makes the main decisions about what to use.
● Draw around the plate on to the sugar paper and invite your child to think of this as her 'face'.
● When she has completed her dressing up and is happy with her outfit, ask her to decorate her 'face' with felt-tipped pens, as she would like it to look. You will then do your best to recreate this on her real face, using the face-paints.
● Show her the finished result using a hand mirror and then encourage her to look at herself in a long mirror.
● Is she happy with the final result? Does she think she looks like her chosen character?

Taking it further
● Let your child decorate your face or one of her doll's faces with the face-paints.
● Encourage her to think about the effect she wants to produce. Is the character happy or sad, young or old?

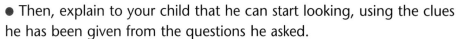

INDOOR GAMES

SENSES COVERED
Sight, hearing.

LEARNING OPPORTUNITY
● To ask questions and follow up answers.

YOU WILL NEED
A teddy; tambourine.

 STEPPING STONE Respond to simple instructions.

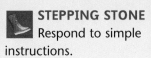 **EARLY LEARNING GOAL**
Communication, language and literacy: Sustain attentive listening, responding to what they have heard by relevant comments, questions or actions.

Hide-and-seek

Sharing the game

● Explain that you will be playing a game where you hide the teddy and your child has to try to find him, by asking you questions and then looking very carefully.

● Choose one room in which to play the game so that you limit the number of possible hiding places.

● Tell your child that he can ask you two questions about where the teddy might be, before he starts looking.

● The type of question should be very general to begin with, for example, 'Is teddy in a cupboard?' or, 'Is he low down or high up?' and so on.

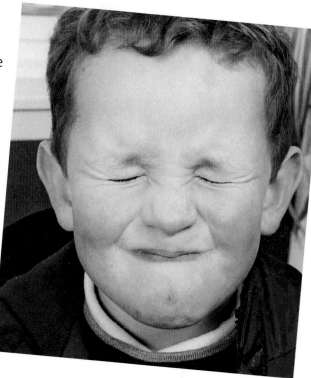

● Then, explain to your child that he can start looking, using the clues he has been given from the questions he asked.

● If necessary, you can help your child to find the teddy by tapping a tambourine very loudly when he is near the toy and quietly when he is far away from it.

Taking it further

● Make the game harder by using several rooms as possible hiding places.

● Allow your child five questions when playing this version of the game so that he can narrow down possibilities, but explain that he cannot ask you which room the teddy is in.

● You may need to help your child to think of suitable questions.

SENSES COVERED
Sight.

LEARNING OPPORTUNITY
● To practise putting puzzles together.

YOU WILL NEED
Bright A4 pictures with clear detail and lots of different colours; colour photocopies of the pictures (if possible); thick black felt-tipped pens; PVA glue; card; scissors.

STEPPING STONE
Use lines to enclose a space, then begin to use these shapes to represent objects.

EARLY LEARNING GOAL
Creative development: Explore colour, texture, shape, form and space in two dimensions.

Puzzles

Sharing the game
● Explain to your child that she is going to make her own puzzles and then practise putting them together.
● Let your child choose one of the A4 pictures. Ask her to stick it on to some card and allow it to dry.
● Invite her to draw two black lines across the picture and another two down it, dividing the picture into nine sections. It does not matter if the lines are not totally horizontal or vertical; in fact it will make the puzzle more interesting if they are not.
● Help your child to cut along the dividing lines carefully, collecting all the pieces of the puzzle together.
● When she has all the pieces assembled, encourage her to look very closely at the photocopy of the picture, in order to work out how to put the pieces together and complete the puzzle.
● Store the photocopy of the finished picture and the puzzle pieces in a suitable box.

Taking it further
● Encourage your child to produce more complicated puzzles by dividing the pictures into more pieces (for example, instead of two lines both across and down the picture, ask her to draw three, giving sixteen pieces).
● Alternatively, show her how to draw random shapes on the picture so that the image is divided into ten or more sections.
● Use photocopies of photographs of family members or pets to make puzzles.

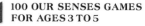

SENSES COVERED
Sight.

LEARNING OPPORTUNITY
● To understand how shadows are formed.

YOU WILL NEED
Large torch or table lamp; teddy; light coloured wall in a darkened room.

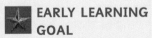

STEPPING STONE
Use their bodies to explore space.

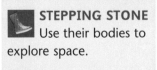

EARLY LEARNING GOAL
Creative development: Explore shape, form and space in two dimensions.

Shadows

Sharing the game
● Show your child how a dark shadow is formed on the pale wall when the teddy is placed in front of the torch or lamp.
● Explain to your child that he is going to be a puppeteer, entertaining you with different-shaped shadows that are doing different things.
● He is going to move his hands in front of the light source, in order to make the various shapes.
● Demonstrate how he can lock his two thumbs together with his other fingers outstretched to make a shadow that looks like a bird.
● Show him how his pointed index finger, when waggled up and down, looks like a wiggly worm.
● Encourage your child to experiment with his hands and fingers in other positions, looking carefully as he moves to see what shapes these make.
● When he has settled on various good shadows, let him work out a show using the different characters, animals or objects that he can make.

Taking it further
● Let him try placing other objects in front of the light to see what type of shadows these give.
● Experiment with moving the objects nearer to and further away from the light. What difference does this make?
● Share the rhyme 'Now the day is over' from page 126.

SENSES COVERED
Sight, touch.

LEARNING OPPORTUNITY
● To create something beautiful.

YOU WILL NEED
Various collage pieces, for example, sequins, wool, shiny paper, balsa wood offcuts, pasta, silver foil, cotton-wool; poster paint; brushes; PVA glue; card.

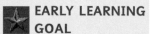 **STEPPING STONE**
Make collages and paintings.

EARLY LEARNING GOAL
Creative development: Explore colour, texture, shape, form and space in two or three dimensions.

My special picture

Sharing the game
● Invite your child to make a present for someone special who likes pictures. This might be a friend or family member.
● Talk about the different ways of creating pleasing effects.
● Look together at the various collage pieces. Note the contrasting shapes, colours and textures.

● Now look at the different-coloured poster paints and let your child decide what colour she would like for the background to her picture. She might like to mix the different paints to produce a new colour.
● Let her paint the card her chosen colour. When the paint is dry, paint over it again with watered-down PVA glue. This will prevent the paint from running when the collage pieces are stuck on to it and will also give a pleasing shiny finish.
● When the card is totally dry, encourage your child to stick on the collage pieces to create the effect she wants. If she decides on flowers, for instance, she could use a small cotton-wool ball for the centre of the flower, with pieces of pasta for the petals.
● Encourage her to really look at her emerging picture as she is doing it, to see if she likes the effect that is being produced. If not, how can she alter it?

Taking it further
● Encourage your child to come up with other ideas for collage pieces on pictures.
● Look at other ways of creating pretty collage effects (such as paper weaving, plaiting and so on).

LEARNING OPPORTUNITY
● To learn to look at things very carefully.

YOU WILL NEED
A large tray; collection of objects, some small, some a little larger, which can be placed on the tray.

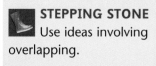
STEPPING STONE
Use ideas involving overlapping.

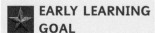
EARLY LEARNING GOAL
Creative development: Explore shape in two and three dimensions.

The tray game

Sharing the game
● Prepare the tray by putting quite a few objects on it and arranging them so that some are partially covering others.
● In this game, your child will be able to look at the tray all the time, but some of the objects will be covered up with other ones and he will have to look very carefully to see what is there.
● Explain that he must not move anything.
● Invite him to name as many things as he can. Write down his answers as he gives them.
● After a while, when it seems your child has had enough, remove the named objects one by one and see if anything is left.
● As you do this, encourage your child to tell you anything else that he notices.

Taking it further
● Draw three or four simple objects in different-coloured felt-tipped pens, slightly overlapping one another. Can your child name everything you have drawn?
● Cover various large, distinctively shaped objects (for example, a ball, a box and a doll) with thin material. Can your child identify the objects just by looking at the shapes under the material?

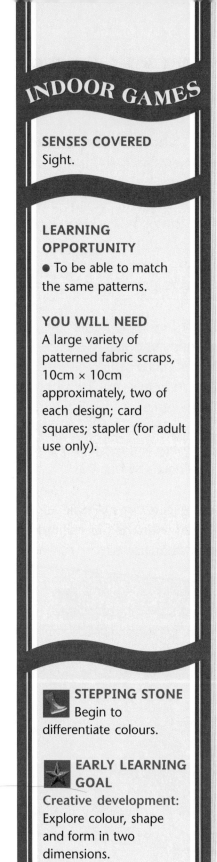
SENSES COVERED
Sight.

LEARNING OPPORTUNITY
● To be able to match the same patterns.

YOU WILL NEED
A large variety of patterned fabric scraps, 10cm × 10cm approximately, two of each design; card squares; stapler (for adult use only).

STEPPING STONE
Begin to differentiate colours.

EARLY LEARNING GOAL
Creative development: Explore colour, shape and form in two dimensions.

Snap!

Sharing the game

● Staple all the fabric squares on to different cards. Divide the cards into two 'packs', each containing one of the fabric samples.

● Discuss the various sorts of patterns found on clothing (yours and your child's), noticing different colours, types and size of patterns.

● Explain to your child that you are going to play a game which involves her matching up pieces of fabric.

● Show her that all the fabric pieces are stapled on to thin card and then divided into two packs. Both of the packs will contain the same fabric samples.

● Mix up the cards and give one pack to your child. Keep the other yourself.

● Turn over one of your cards on to the table in front of you.

● As your child turns over her card, she must look to see if it is the same as yours or different. If it is the same, she must say, 'Snap'. She then picks up the cards and  takes another turn. If it is not, you must turn over another card. If yours is the same as hers, you say, 'Snap'.

Taking it further

● Try playing traditional 'Snap' with a normal pack of playing cards. This time, your child will have to recognise cards which are almost the same, but not exactly.

● Explain that for the number cards, she will have to look at numerals and the number of objects, rather than their shapes.

● For the royal cards, she will have to look at the letters and the type of person in the picture.

SENSES COVERED
Sight.

LEARNING OPPORTUNITY
● To be able to identify different shapes and match them up.

YOU WILL NEED
Large plastic or card shapes (a triangle, circle, square and rectangle); picture books or colour magazines.

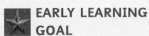

STEPPING STONE Show curiosity and observation by talking about shapes, how they are the same or why some are different.

EARLY LEARNING GOAL Mathematical development: Use language such as 'circle' or 'bigger' to describe the shape and size of flat shapes.

Find that shape!

Sharing the game
● Explain to your child that this game involves matching up different shapes with objects or pictures of objects.
● Show your child the different shape templates and talk through the names of these.
● Discuss together real things that are that shape.
● Point out the fact that shapes can be all different sizes. For example, rectangles can be long and thin as well as short and fat.
● Triangles must have three sides, but can still look very different. Some are tall and pointed while others are wide and flat.
● Give your child one of the shapes and challenge him to find as many pictures as he can of things which are that kind of shape.
● Make the game more complicated by asking your child to find things of a specific shape and colour.
● If your child is easily rising to the challenge, ask him to find things of a specific shape, colour and size.
● Repeat the game with each shape.

Taking it further
● Look for other shapes as well – for example, a squashed circle (an oval) and a hexagon.
● Play a similar game when out and about. Look for shapes in the real world, such as rectangular doors, circular traffic signs, triangular roofs and so on.

SENSES COVERED
Touch.

LEARNING OPPORTUNITY
● To be able to carry a number of things without dropping them.

YOU WILL NEED
Soft toys; balls; empty boxes of different sizes; fabric pieces.

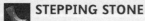
THINK FIRST!
Make sure you try this game when no one is in the way or at risk of getting hurt.

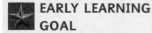
STEPPING STONE
Persevere in repeating some actions/ attempts when developing a new skill.

EARLY LEARNING GOAL
Physical development: Show an awareness of space.

Steady!

Sharing the game
● Explain to your child that this game is about trying to balance several things on top of each other. You are going to challenge her to carry as much as she possibly can without dropping anything.

● Look carefully at the items you have collected.
● Note the different size and shape of the boxes. Will it be better to balance a smaller box on top of a bigger one or the other way around? Let her experiment, in order to work out which method works best.
● Try putting one of the balls directly on a smooth floor. What happens? Point out the curved edges which make the rounded ball roll.
● Now try putting the ball on a crumpled piece of fabric. What happens? Note how the folds of the material keep the ball in one place and stop it from rolling.
● How will your child be able to stop the balls rolling around when she tries to carry everything?
● Look at the soft toys and notice how their floppy bodies make a rough surface which will hold the balls in place.
● After this initial discussion, challenge your child to tell you how to load her up, so that she can carry lots of items in her arms without dropping them. She must tell you which item she wants you to give her next and where exactly she wants you to put it.

Taking it further
● After your child's first attempt, count the number of items she managed to successfully hold and see if she can improve her total when she tries again.
● Share the traditional rhyme 'Humpty Dumpty'.

SENSES COVERED
Hearing.

LEARNING OPPORTUNITY
● To practise listening carefully.

YOU WILL NEED
Group of children.

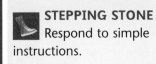 **STEPPING STONE** Respond to simple instructions.

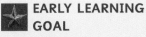 **EARLY LEARNING GOAL**
Communication, language and literacy: Sustain attentive listening, responding to what they have heard by relevant actions.

Chinese whispers

Sharing the game
● Play this game with your child and a group of his friends.
● Discuss the importance of listening very carefully so that the children understand what is being asked of them.
● Give examples of how messages can get confused if people do not listen carefully, for example, if you have asked your child to 'find the cat' and he 'brings you his hat'.
● Sit the children down in a circle.
● Explain that you will whisper an instruction (for example, 'Please close the door'), once only, to one child in the group. They will then have to whisper this message on to the next child in the circle.
● Pass the message around the circle in this way until it reaches the last child.
● Ask this child to carry out the instruction, if it still makes sense.
● Having seen the action, ask the first child if that was the instruction he was given by you.
● If it was, repeat the game with another message and a different child beginning the process of relaying the message.
● If it was not, see if the children can improve their listening skills by trying again.
● In the unlikely event that the instruction was misheard right at the beginning of the game, you will have to say what it was. Discuss how it might have been misheard.

Taking it further
● Make the initial instruction more complicated, perhaps involving two or three elements, for example, 'Please put my book on the shelf, push the chair under the table and close the door'.

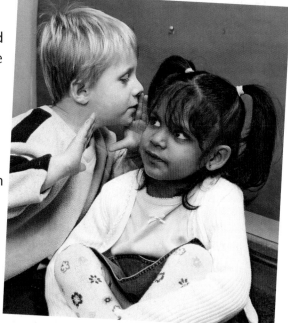

SENSES COVERED
Touch.

LEARNING OPPORTUNITY
● To use the sense of touch constructively.

YOU WILL NEED
Sheet of thick A3 card; material for the rabbit's body (velvet for his ears, fluffy for his body, smooth for his nose); crumpled silver foil for claws; plastic eye; cotton-wool balls; sticky-backed Velcro; thick fish-gut wire; a fine skewer; PVA glue; sticky tape; scissors; felt-tipped pen; blindfold.

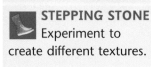

STEPPING STONE
Experiment to create different textures.

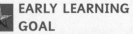

EARLY LEARNING GOAL
Creative development: Explore texture and shape in two or three dimensions.

Pin the tail on the rabbit

Sharing the game
● Stick a small piece of the hooked side of the Velcro on to the cotton-wool ball to make the rabbit's tail.
● Draw a large rabbit on to the A3 card.
● Cut out material shapes for the rabbit's body and help your child to stick them on to the drawing, so that the rabbit has a fluffy body, velvety ears, sharp claws and a smooth nose.

● Stick the eye in position and draw on his mouth.
● Pierce three holes in the card for whiskers, using the skewer.
● Thread fish-gut wire through these holes, fastening them to the back of the card with sticky tape.
● When the rabbit is totally dry, let your child feel him, encouraging her to think about where the various features of the rabbit are and, therefore, where the different textures are in relation to each other.
● Blindfold your child, give her the rabbit tail and ask her to place it in the correct position, using only her sense of touch.
● Repeat the game to see if she can improve on the tail's position.

Taking it further
● Paint a carrot and some grass on to card. When dry, stick on pieces of Velcro, and invite your child to put the carrot in the rabbit's mouth and the grass under his feet, again by using her sense of touch only.

SENSES COVERED
Touch, sight.

LEARNING OPPORTUNITY
● To learn that magnets attract metal.

YOU WILL NEED
Sand-pit; large magnet; selection of ten small objects – some metal (attracted to the magnet) and some plastic.

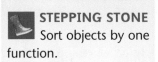
STEPPING STONE
Sort objects by one function.

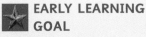
EARLY LEARNING GOAL
Knowledge and understanding of the world: Ask questions about why things happen and how things work.

Lucky dip

Sharing the game
● Show your child the magnet and demonstrate how it is attracted to the metal objects in your selection.
● Run the magnet over the top of the sand to show that it is not attracted to the sand itself.
● Ask your child to help you to bury all the objects in the sand-pit. Make sure that they are not visible, but some should be nearer the surface of the sand than others. Check that you can see nothing poking out of the sand.
● Explain that you are now going to play a 'Lucky dip' game, in which your child has to feel for the objects in the sand with his fingers. When he finds something, he can wipe some of the sand off the bit he has found, but must not remove the whole object from the sand-pit.
● Can he tell you what the object is, just by feeling the bit he has found? Will this particular object be attracted to the magnet? Can he explain why, or why not?
● Invite him to try to remove the object with his magnet. If it is metal, it should stick to the magnet when it comes close and lift easily out of the sand.
● Take it in turns to have a 'dip'. Score one point for each object removed from the sand by the magnet. After three turns, count together who has the most points.

Taking it further
● Bury three larger, easily recognised objects in the sand without your child seeing. Can he tell you what they are by touch alone?

SENSES COVERED
Smell, touch.

LEARNING OPPORTUNITY
● To be able to match several different smells.

YOU WILL NEED
Play dough; food colouring in green, blue, red and yellow; peppermint essence; vanilla essence; lemon juice; perfume.

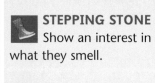 **STEPPING STONE**
Show an interest in what they smell.

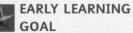 **EARLY LEARNING GOAL**
Creative development: Respond in a variety of ways to what they smell.

Match the smell

Sharing the game
● Divide the play dough into four. Roll it into balls and flatten. Put a few drops of the food colouring in the middle of each portion – a different colour for each – and fold the dough over. Gradually work the colour into the dough. When the colour is absorbed, let your child help to work it in, enjoying the feel of the flexible dough.
● Now divide each of the coloured portions into two, creating eight little balls of dough.
● Without your child seeing, work one of the four flavourings into each of these balls, using each flavouring twice. Add the flavourings randomly to the coloured dough balls.
● Explain that you want your child to play a matching-up game, where she has to find two balls of dough which smell the same.
● At first, she may be tempted to match balls of the same colour, using her sense of sight.
● With encouragement, however, she should be able to ignore the colour and concentrate on her sense of smell instead.
● At the end of the game, she should have four separate pairs of dough balls, representing four different smells.

Taking it further
● Help your child to roll out another quantity of play dough and let her cut out four different shapes – two of each.
● Without her looking, put a few drops of the smell on each shape – again using each smell twice and using the shapes randomly.
● This time, your child will have to ignore the shapes involved to concentrate on matching the smells.

CHAPTER 5

Sharing new and traditional stories, nursery rhymes and songs with your child can be an immensely rewarding experience for both of you. It is a time when your child knows he has your full and undivided attention, and it can provide a wonderful, natural opportunity for you to increase your child's concentration and imaginative skills. Your child will want to sit still and listen carefully as he is entertained by your storytelling, sharing well-loved and new texts together.

The games in this chapter focus mainly on the sense of hearing, but there are also games relating to the other four senses, as special time is spent together at the end of the day.

TOGETHER TIME

LISTENING

At the age of three, most children can only concentrate for short periods of time. The majority will quickly lose interest in what they are doing and find it hard to sit still and listen. Most of the time, they are making a fair bit of noise themselves and will have to be encouraged to stop, be silent and really listen hard to what is going on around them. They may cope with simple instructions, but will probably find it hard to remember what they have been told is going to happen during the day and will need to be told repeatedly. By the time they reach the age of four, their concentration span should be increasing and they will be more aware of what is going on around them. They can listen carefully, will be keen to respond to requests for help and should be able to convey messages successfully from one person to another. By the time they reach five years old, they will hopefully be sufficiently interested in what is happening so they will be able to remind you what you said, rather than the other way around!

How you can help
● Make sure you take your child for his regular hearing checks. If, in between times, you are at all worried about your child's ability to hear, you should immediately take it up with your doctor.

● Play simple games with your child to increase concentration, for example, 'I went shopping and I bought…'. Take it in turns to add items to the list and remember what has gone before.
● Talk to your child in one-to-one situations, especially about things which capture his imagination.
● When your child is playing, give him sufficient help to allow him to stay engaged on a task, such as completing a puzzle.
● To encourage your child to be able to sit still, get him used to sitting down and waiting while you bring him his meal, turn on his TV programme and so on, so that he is sitting quietly in anticipation.
● To enable your child to practise responding to more complicated instructions, ask him to do several things, one after the other, for example, 'Please put the bricks away in that box and put the books on that shelf'.
● Be patient about repeating yourself!

MUSIC, RHYMES AND STORIES

At the age of three, children enjoy listening to favourite songs, rhymes and stories over and over again, and will join in with key phrases, relevant animal noises and so on. At four years old, they are ready to sing a number of songs, including some new ones, sometimes playing instruments to accompany them. They will also be able to make up some of their own songs. Longer and more challenging stories can be introduced, but, as part of a regular routine, they should still be read familiar stories, chant familiar rhymes and have the opportunity to sing thoroughly familiar songs. At the age of five, children start to learn a wide variety of new songs, and will be interested in different types of music. They can be encouraged to express a view as to which songs, rhymes and stories they enjoy, and be given the chance to choose which they want to sing or hear.

How you can help
● Provide plenty of opportunities for your child to hear and practise familiar songs and stories.
● Play games where your child has to identify how you have changed the words in a familiar rhyme or song.
● Encourage your child to make up nonsense rhymes for themselves, for example, 'Humpty Dumpty sat on a pin, there was the most terrible din!'.
● Gradually introduce new stories and music – appropriate to your child's mood.
● Talk about the different kinds of music that are around and identify that which is happy, sad, fast, slow and so on.

CREATIVE LANGUAGE SKILLS

Three-year-olds should be able to tell you the outline of a familiar story in their own words. By the time they reach the age of four, they should be able to listen carefully for longer periods of time and should, therefore, be more able to provide details of stories they have heard or suggest suitable endings for new stories being read to them. They will also have a growing vocabulary and may be able to suggest suitable words for sounds they hear. By the age of five, when they are likely to have been in nursery or school for a while, they will be familiar with hearing language used by both adults and children, and will have heard a wide selection of stories and rhymes. This should enable them to predict outcomes, suggest alternatives and use suitable words for describing a number of sounds in various situations.

How you can help
● Listen out for quiet times during the day and point these out to your child, so she gets used to listening to background sounds.
● Encourage your child to listen by talking to her as you go about your daily routine, describing what is happening, what you can see or hear, what you are feeling and so on.
● Use new and interesting language, introducing words your child may not have heard before.
● When you read stories together, ask your child what is happening and what she thinks might happen next, or at the end of the story, how she might change the ending to make it different.

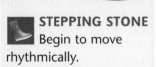
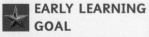
Listen to the music

Sharing the game

● Sit comfortably with your child and listen carefully to some of the relaxing music.

● Help your child to feel the beat by clapping with him in time to the music.

● Pretend to be a conductor and move your hands up and down in time to the music. Encourage your child to copy you, while listening carefully to the music.

● What does the music suggest to him?

● How could he use and move the various parts of his body to illustrate these suggestions?

● Explain that you would like him to move in response to the music, but without getting up.

● Invite him to think up gentle movements with his head, neck, hands, ankles and feet to accompany the music. Encourage his own suggestions, but be ready to help if necessary, for example, if the music makes him think of swans swimming along, show him how to stretch his neck up pretending to be one, as he sways his hand to and fro to the rhythm.

● Share a few ideas for movement of your own with your child to stimulate his imagination.

Taking it further

● Invite your child to use a few different musical instruments, such as a triangle, shakers and a penny whistle to join in with the music. Encourage him to listen very carefully, so that the sound he makes is complementary, rather than destructive.

⦿⦿⦿⦿⦿⦿⦿⦿⦿⦿⦿⦿⦿⦿⦿⦿⦿⦿⦿⦿⦿⦿⦿⦿⦿⦿

On the phone

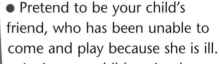

TOGETHER TIME

SENSES COVERED
Hearing.

LEARNING OPPORTUNITY
● To be able to hold a conversation.

YOU WILL NEED
Two toy telephones.

 STEPPING STONE
Initiate conversation, attend to and take account of what others say.

EARLY LEARNING GOAL
Communication, language and literacy: Interact with others, negotiating plans and taking turns in conversation.

Sharing the game
● Explain why we need to use the telephone. Sometimes our friends and family are not with us when we want to talk to them and then the telephone can be a very useful way to keep in touch.

● Pretend to be your child's friend, who has been unable to come and play because she is ill.
● Invite your child to ring her friend and talk to her.
● Encourage your child to initiate the conversation. As her friend is ill, what might be a good thing to ask first? What might she tell her friend to cheer her up? She might like to hear that your child will ask her to play again when she is better.
● Take on the friend's role, replying to your child's questions, but also asking some of your own, for example, 'What have you been doing today?' or, 'What shall we do together when I can come and play?'.

● Encourage your child to listen very carefully to what is being asked and to answer any questions as fully as she can. Help her with follow-up questions, if necessary, if her replies are a little monosyllabic at first. Always ask open-ended questions (that is, ones to which the answer is more than 'yes' or 'no'), to encourage conversation.

Taking it further
● Imagine that Daddy/Mummy is going to be back late tonight. Suggest to your child that she rings to say goodnight. What does she really want to tell him/her about, that has happened today?

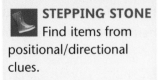
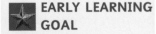
Can you draw it?

Sharing the game

● Choose a simple item for your child to draw. These instructions are for a house.

● Explain that your child needs to listen very carefully to what you are saying and to follow the instructions you will give him.

● Remind him of the shape of a triangle, square and rectangle, and go through the meaning of various positional words, such as up, down, along, above, below and so on.

● Begin the instructions, offering help as necessary, if you see that the shape being drawn is going to be unrecognisable.

● Start by telling him to draw a straight line **along** the bottom of the page.

● Draw a rectangle going **up** the page **in the middle of** this line.

● At each end of this line, draw two long lines **up** the page.

● Draw another line **along** the top of the page joining the **top** of these two lines together.

● **Above** this line, draw a big triangle.

● **On the side of** this triangle, draw a small rectangle.

● **On top of** this rectangle, draw a curly shape.

● Draw four squares **inside** the biggest rectangle, one in each corner.

● Ask your child what he has drawn. At what stage did he know what you were asking him to draw?

Taking it further

● Repeat the instructions for other simple pictures, using different positional words. For example, for a wavy sea – draw a line **up** and **across** the page, then **down** and **across the page**, then **up** and **across** and so on.

○ ○

SENSES COVERED
Hearing, sight.

LEARNING OPPORTUNITY
● To practise counting up and down, while reciting and singing rhymes.

YOU WILL NEED
A book of number rhymes; bricks; eight potatoes; two plastic sausages; frying pan: five plastic buns.

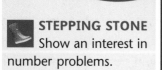

STEPPING STONE
Show an interest in number problems.

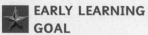

EARLY LEARNING GOAL
Mathematical development: Begin to relate addition to combining two groups of objects and subtraction to 'taking away'.

Number rhymes

Sharing the game
● Practise counting up to ten and down again with your child. Encourage her to listen very carefully to the correct order of the number names.

● Select several rhymes which involve counting up through the numbers, for example, 'One, Two, Three, Four, Five, Once I Caught a Fish Alive' and 'One Potato, Two Potato, Three Potato, Four'.

● Invite your child to listen as you sing and to use bricks to build a tower, adding one more brick as you count up through the numbers. This way she will be able to see the concept of **more** by looking at the tower growing taller, as she hears the numbers getting bigger. Where the rhyme is about specific things (for example, potatoes), encourage her to use those actual props to help her understanding of **more**.

● Now choose some rhymes which concentrate on taking away, for example, 'Five Currant Buns in a Baker's Shop' and 'Two Fat Sausages Sizzling in the Pan'.

● Again, as she listens to the numbers getting smaller, ask her to use the props to see what is happening when she removes one at a time and is left with **less**.

Taking it further
● Make a pile of three bricks. Count them together. How could your child make a pile of five? Encourage her to make a pile of two bricks to add to the three, by pushing them together.

● Make a pile of three bricks and a pile of four. How could she make two piles of three bricks? (Take away one brick from the pile of four.)

SENSES COVERED
Hearing.

LEARNING OPPORTUNITY
● To practise listening very carefully and noticing changes.

YOU WILL NEED
A nursery rhyme book.

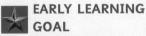 **STEPPING STONE**
Listen to favourite nursery rhymes and songs.

EARLY LEARNING GOAL
Communication, language and literacy: Sustain attentive listening, responding to what they have heard by relevant comments.

Different rhymes

Sharing the game
● This game involves your child listening out very carefully for changes made to familiar rhymes.
● Before you start the game, read or sing the correct versions of the nursery rhymes you plan to use.
● Now read them again, some correctly and some with slight changes made to them.
● Encourage your child to listen out for the changes and to stop you whenever he notices one.
● Alter the rhymes in various ways.
● Put in words opposite in meaning, for example, 'Jack and Jill went **down** the hill'.
● Substitute words similar in meaning, for example, 'Humpty Dumpty **knelt** on a wall, Humpty Dumpty had a **bad** fall'.
● Substitute words with the exact same meaning, for example, 'Jack and Jill went up the hill to fetch a **bucket** of water'.
● Use words which sound roughly the same, for example, 'Twinkle, twinkle **pretty** star, **oh** I wonder what you are'.

● The differences should be as subtle as possible, so that your child has to listen really hard.
● Use rhymes involving counting down as well, such as the song 'Five Little Speckled Frogs'. Then, say the wrong number as you count down (for example, three instead of four frogs in the second verse), to see if your child notices.
● Reverse roles and see if he can make mistakes for you to notice.

Taking it further
● As well as noticing your mistakes, see if your child can repeat the rhyme with the changes you made, instead of the correct rhyme.

SENSES COVERED
Hearing, sight.

LEARNING OPPORTUNITY
● To find words to describe different sounds.

YOU WILL NEED
A bath or basin within reach of your child.

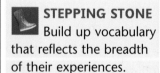 **THINK FIRST!** Watch out for very hot water coming from the hot tap. Always supervise your child closely when using water.

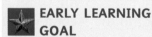 **STEPPING STONE** Build up vocabulary that reflects the breadth of their experiences.

EARLY LEARNING GOAL Communication, language and literacy: Extend their vocabulary, exploring the meanings and sounds of new words.

Bathtime

Sharing the game
● Encourage your child to turn on the taps carefully and start filling the bath or basin.
● As the water is running in, encourage her to come up with words to describe the sound the water is making. If necessary, help her with a few suggestions (rushing, splashing and so on).
● How does the sound change when the taps are turned on only a little? Again, ask her to think of words to describe the sound (trickling, dripping and so on).
● Notice the difference in the speed of filling the bath or basin when the taps are full or half on.
● Encourage your child to play with the water, to see if she can produce any other sounds. What words would she use to describe these sounds?
● Finally, let your child pull the plug out and listen carefully as the water disappears. Can she hear any gurgling noises?
● Invite her to watch out for the water swirling around the plughole when the bath or basin is nearly empty.

Taking it further
● Suggest that your child puts some bubble bath into the bath or basin as the tap is running. Watch how frothy bubbles appear very quickly when the taps are full on, but are not as obvious when the water is running slowly. Listen out for the sound of the bubbles bursting and ask her for words to describe the noise.
● Is there a difference in the smell of the water with and without bubble bath?

SENSES COVERED
Hearing.

LEARNING OPPORTUNITY
● To learn and enjoy singing a variety of songs connected with water.

YOU WILL NEED
A bath or basin within reach of your child; other props depending on the songs chosen (for example, a toy kettle, bucket, plastic frogs and ducks).

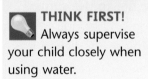

THINK FIRST!
Always supervise your child closely when using water.

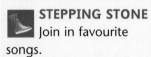

STEPPING STONE
Join in favourite songs.

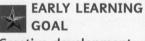

EARLY LEARNING GOAL
Creative development: Sing simple songs from memory.

Bathtime songs

Sharing the game

● Sing through some of the songs your child knows well, asking him to remember ones which are linked to water in any way, for example, 'Row, Row, Row Your Boat', 'Polly Put the Kettle On', 'Jack and Jill', 'Five Little Speckled Frogs' or 'Five Little Ducks Went Swimming One Day' and so on.

● When you have chosen two or three songs, ask your child to come up with suitable actions to accompany them.

● Sing through the songs and mime the actions.

● Now consider those songs again. How could your child alter the actions so that he is using the water in the bath or basin?

● Encourage him to use his hands in the water to 'row' his imaginary boat, to actually fill the kettle or bucket with water from the tap, to make the frogs jump into the bath or basin of water, and to swim the ducks along.

● As he does all these actions 'for real', encourage him to think of the noises associated with them (swirling, splattering, plopping, swishing and so on).

Taking it further

● Can he invent his own song, using his own 'noisy' words, to accompany some of the sounds he is making while he is playing with the water?

● Share the rhyme 'Polly put the kettle on' on page 127 with your child, and ask him to sing along.

LEARNING OPPORTUNITY
● To identify the feel of various items used in the bathroom.

YOU WILL NEED
A variety of soaps, oils, shampoos and bubble bath; a doll; bath or basin within reach of your child.

THINK FIRST!
Always supervise your child closely when using water.

STEPPING STONE
Show an interest in what they touch.

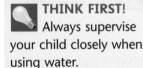

EARLY LEARNING GOAL
Creative development: Respond in a variety of ways to what they touch.

A nice feeling

Sharing the game

● Explain that soaps make our skin clean, while shampoos make our hair clean. Oils help to keep our skin soft and supple, while bubble bath provides lots of bubbles in the bath water.

● Help your child to discover that soap forms a lather much more easily in warm water. Soap that has been in cold water remains rather hard and almost sticky, whereas soap that has been in warm water becomes soft and has a rather slimy feel. When the softened soap is rubbed between her hands, it produces a creamy lather which cleans her skin.

● Encourage your child to rub some oil into her clean skin. It will feel greasy and wet, but will soon be absorbed into the skin, leaving it soft and smooth.

● Invite her to use some shampoo on her doll's hair. Ask her to rub it in gently and let her feel the foamy result. When it is rinsed off, the hair will feel 'squeaky' clean.

● Create a wonderfully bubbly environment by swirling the bubble bath around in running water. Let your child feel the result and tell you why she thinks this might be nice to lie in.

Taking it further

● Invite your child to try getting a lather with soap in salty water. Notice that no matter how hard she rubs, very little lather appears.

● Explain that in order to wash in salty sea water, we need to use special soap.

Cleaning teeth

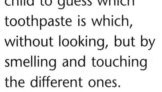

Sharing the game

● Look together at the various toothpastes. Try to have collected one which is a white paste, one which is a blue gel, one which is stripy and one children's paste in a fruity flavour. Examine both the packaging and the contents of the tube, noting the differences.

● Smell the contents of each tube, having examined the outside, identifying the minty adult pastes and the fruity children's one.

● Squirt a little toothpaste out of each tube on to a plate. Let your child touch each one to see if he can detect any difference in the textures.

● Explain that you are now going to ask your child to guess which toothpaste is which, without looking, but by smelling and touching the different ones.

● Number the tubes from one to four. Tell your child to close his eyes and hand him the first tube. Let him smell the contents and then squirt a small amount on to his hand to feel it.

● When he thinks he has identified it, let him wash his hands and repeat the process with the other tubes. Allow him to smell and feel again if he needs more time.

● Compare your child's guesses with the actual tubes. Did he identify them correctly?

Taking it further

● Why does your child think the children's toothpaste is made in a fruity flavour and has more attractive packaging?

● Which toothpaste does he like best? Encourage him to use it to clean his teeth after this game.

TOGETHER TIME

SENSES COVERED
Sight, smell, touch.

LEARNING OPPORTUNITY
● To encourage a willingness to clean their own teeth.

YOU WILL NEED
A selection of four different toothpastes; plate; sticky labels; felt-tipped pen.

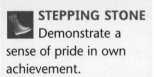 **STEPPING STONE**
Demonstrate a sense of pride in own achievement.

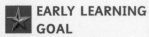 **EARLY LEARNING GOAL**
Personal, social and emotional development: Manage their own personal hygiene.

SENSES COVERED
Hearing, sight.

LEARNING OPPORTUNITY
● To be able to tell a story in their own words.

YOU WILL NEED
A simple story book, but one with lots of detail and plenty of illustrations.

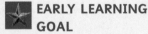 **STEPPING STONE**
Begin to be aware of the way stories are structured.

EARLY LEARNING GOAL
Communication, language and literacy: Retell narratives in the correct sequence, drawing on language patterns of stories.

Storytime

Sharing the game
● Tell your child that you will be reading her a story. She needs to listen very carefully, because you will be asking her to tell you the same story afterwards.

● Make sure that you are both comfortable and look at the book together.
● Talk about the pictures and how they will add to her understanding and enjoyment of the story.
● Read the story to your child, letting her help you to turn the pages.
● As the story progresses, discuss what is happening in each of the pictures, who the main characters are, whether they are 'good' or 'bad' characters, where the story is taking place and how she thinks the story might end.
● When you have finished the story, ask your child whether she enjoyed it. Why (or why not)?
● Now encourage her to tell you the story without referring to the book, trying to remember the order in which things happened and as much detail as she can.
● Prompt as necessary.

Taking it further
● When your child has had a go at remembering the story, tell it again yourself, making a few deliberate mistakes. See if she can correct you by remembering any of the details you have 'forgotten'.

LEARNING OPPORTUNITY
● To use their imagination to create sounds to represent actions or events.

YOU WILL NEED
A selection of musical instruments; saucepan lids; wooden spoons; newspaper; silver foil; hand bell; plastic bottle half-full of water; hand brush; coins or any other suitable props for your chosen story.

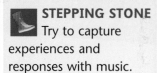
STEPPING STONE
Try to capture experiences and responses with music.

EARLY LEARNING GOAL
Creative development: Express and communicate their ideas, thoughts and feelings by using a widening range of materials, suitable tools, imaginative and role-play and musical instruments.

Story sounds

Sharing the game
● Choose a suitable story with lots of different ideas for possible sound effects, for example, a story with animal or bird sounds, involving noisy children, stormy weather or including sounds of the seaside and so on.

● In this game, your child has to work out how to imitate the sounds in the story by using some of the instruments or other props you have collected.
● Read your chosen story together, identifying where you feel it is appropriate to add sound effects. Choose five or six sounds to illustrate.
● Encourage your child to think carefully about the sort of sound he wants to produce. Is it high or low? Is it soft or loud? Is it long or short? Does he want to scare you or make you feel happy?
● Let him experiment as much as necessary and, when he is happy with the various sounds he wants to create, gather all the props he needs into one place.
● Enjoy giving a 'performance' of the story. Read it slowly, indicating to your child when he should make the sounds.

Taking it further
● Ask your child to try making sound effects using parts of his body only, for example, stamping his feet, drumming his fingers on the table, clapping his hands, sighing, humming and so on.

SENSES COVERED
Hearing.

LEARNING OPPORTUNITY
● To learn that, even when your child is totally silent, there are still lots of noises going on around her.

YOU WILL NEED
No special requirements.

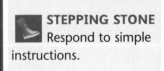
STEPPING STONE
Respond to simple instructions.

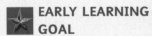
EARLY LEARNING GOAL
Communication, language and literacy: Sustain attentive listening, responding to what they have heard by relevant comments.

What can you hear?

Sharing the game

● Explain how we usually 'switch off' to background noises as we are too busy doing other things. The purpose of this game is for your child to listen very carefully to see what she can hear going on around her, when she is totally silent and not doing anything else.

● Encourage at least one minute of silence, asking your child to notice what she hears, but to say nothing until the minute is over.

● When the minute is up, invite her to tell you all the different sounds that she heard.

● Depending on your setting, these sounds might include clocks ticking, radios, adult voices, children's voices, traffic, aeroplanes, wind, rain, doors shutting or opening, birds singing and so on.

● If your child comes up with only a few sounds she has heard, repeat the minute's silence and see if she can hear anything else.

● If necessary, tell her what sounds to listen out for and see if she can hear it now.

Taking it further

● Put on a nursery rhyme tape quietly in the background as you read your child an exciting story. When you have finished, ask her what nursery rhymes she heard. Hopefully, she will not be able to tell you as she will have been listening too hard to the story and will have ignored the background noise.

CHAPTER 6

The five senses of sight, hearing, smell, taste and touch are enormously important in helping children to become more aware of what is going on around them. Children are naturally curious, and careful use of all their senses helps them to learn more as they explore the environment in which they live. This eventually leads to having a greater understanding of the world around them. Like all new skills, learning to use all of their senses to maximum effect so that they can be really useful to them, will take lots of time and practice.

The games in this chapter concentrate on developing keen senses as children have fun on visits and playing out of doors.

OUTDOOR FUN

SENSORY DELIGHTS

Very young children like to be surrounded by familiarity. They can easily feel threatened by any break in their routine. It takes time for three-year-olds to accept new experiences as exciting opportunities, with the potential to give enormous pleasure. At the age of four, most children find it easier to accept unfamiliar places, people and situations, and can appreciate that many of these will soon become part of their normal experience, adding to their enjoyment. By the time they reach the age of five, when children become much better at using all of their senses to the full, their familiar world expands dramatically and they are able to explore, enjoy, understand and appreciate fully an enormous number of different things.

especially the features of different environments.
● Look out for variation in individual colours, especially in the natural world.
● Point out shapes and patterns, noting how often these are visible in different buildings.
● Play your child a wide variety of music so that he has the opportunity to express a view about what he would like to hear.
● Encourage him to listen very carefully to what you are saying and to the other noises surrounding him. Try to avoid loud background noise.
● Invite your child to use his sense of touch at every opportunity, especially when examining living things, to help him to explore objects and to add to his enjoyment.
● Encourage him to notice cooking smells and to enjoy the taste that goes with them.

How you can help
● Make sure your child understands the role of his eyes in helping him to see; his ears in helping him to hear; his nose in helping him to smell; his fingers in helping him to touch, and his tongue in helping him to taste.
● Encourage him to notice detail when you are out and about,

SENSORY CHANGES

Three-year-olds expect their familiar world to be a certain way and they want it to stay that way. Most will not be very interested in change. Four-year-olds will probably be more flexible. They should be able to accept that slight changes (for example, different-shaped fish fingers) are unlikely to make a great difference (to their taste), whereas more noticeable changes (for example, fish which smells nasty) may well suggest trouble (a stomach upset). They will be able to understand that one spot on the face does not indicate illness, whereas a rash does. Most five-year-olds will be intrigued by changes to familiar things. They will be only too anxious to tell you about the bread which has gone mouldy or the baby's skin which looks sore.

How you can help

● Help your child make the connection between facial expressions and feelings. How does your child's face change with her mood?

● Involve your child in checking that food is still fit to eat, looking at it carefully, smelling it and touching it.
● Let her accompany you as you investigate strange noises to see what is causing them.
● Encourage her to be involved in looking after younger siblings and to be aware of changes that take place as a baby grows up.
● When another family member is ill, explain what has changed to make them feel unwell. This might include a raised temperature, a rash, a cold, a dry mouth and so on.
● Introduce different foods on regular occasions, so that your child gets used to tasting a good variety.
● Encourage her to always be aware of anything that appears to be odd or out of the ordinary.

SENSORY DANGERS

Three-year-olds need to be protected from potential dangers. It is unlikely that they will notice there is a ball on the bottom step of the stairs ready to trip them up, or that their food is too hot to eat. When they reach the age of four, they need to be encouraged to think for themselves and to be more aware of what potentially poses a threat to them. Most four-year-olds are still somewhat unpredictable, so concentrating on their senses will help them to notice dangers. At the age of five, most children can understand why they must or must not do certain things. They are also capable of learning preventative measures, such as the Green Cross Code, and can understand the message never to play near water on their own. A number of five-year-olds will be ready to absorb important information about what to do in an emergency.

How you can help

● Take care not to frighten your child by telling him too much.
● Concentrate on discussing the major dangers which could easily be a threat to your child.
● When taking your child out on the busy street, make sure he holds your hand and knows how to cross the road safely. Never let him play near the street on his own.
● Make sure your child is aware of the dangers of water. When he is playing near water, ensure you are always close at hand.
● Tell your child how important it is to be extremely careful when he is helping you in the kitchen. There are many dangers here, the most obvious being pans full of boiling water. Make sure he stands at a safe distance when you have a pan in your hand and that pan handles are always pointing inwards on the hob.
● Fire is potentially very dangerous. Point out the smell of burning toast, candles burning and bonfires, so that your child will be able to recognise this smell again.

OUTDOOR FUN

SENSES COVERED
Hearing.

LEARNING OPPORTUNITY
● To identify the parts of the body that are connected with the different senses.

YOU WILL NEED
No special requirements.

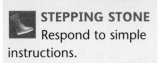
STEPPING STONE
Respond to simple instructions.

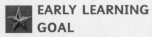
EARLY LEARNING GOAL
Communication, language and literacy: Sustain attentive listening, responding to what they have heard by relevant actions.

What are my senses?

Sharing the game
● Talk to your child about the five different senses, linking each sense to the part of the body with which it is associated.
● To the music of 'Hot Cross Buns', sing sensory rhymes, such as:

Smell the rose,	Feel the fur,	Taste the cake,
Smell the rose,	Feel the fur,	Taste the cake,
You can smell it,	You can touch it,	You can taste it,
I can smell it,	I can touch it,	I can taste it,
With my nose.	With my hand.	With my tongue.

● Substitute words to bring in actions which involve using the other senses as well, for example, cars, planes and birds (for hearing); trees and clouds (for seeing); fruit and cheese (for tasting); sand and grass (for touching); and smoke and buns (for smelling).
● As you sing the words, ask your child to respond by touching the part of his body which enables him to taste, hear, feel, smell and see.
● Include plenty of examples, mixing up the senses so your child has to think carefully about the part of his body he should be pointing to.
● Further emphasise which part of the body is involved in which action by reciting the rhyme 'My eyes can see' on page 127.

Taking it further
● Look at various illustrations in picture books. Discuss what your child would be able to see, hear, touch, taste and feel if he were a character in the story.
● Ask your child to imagine that he is at the seaside/in the park/in his kitchen at home. What can he see, hear, smell, taste and feel?

SENSES COVERED
Sight.

LEARNING OPPORTUNITY
● To learn how to look very carefully and notice detail.

YOU WILL NEED
No special requirements.

 STEPPING STONE Notice differences between features of the local environment.

EARLY LEARNING GOAL
Knowledge and understanding of the world: Observe, find out about and identify features in the place they live.

Remember the way home

Sharing the game

● Talk about your child's sense of sight and how it enables her to see all the wonderful things around her.

● Take her on a short 'memory trail' near her home or school. Explain that you are going to lead her on the way out, but on the way back, you would like her to lead you.

● Before you leave, ask your child how she will recognise her starting-point. Invite her to tell you what she will be looking out for.

● On the outward journey, encourage her to notice as much as she can, especially looking out for trees and flowers, buildings of different types and colours, shops, street signs, bus stops and so on. Ask her to note those things which are particularly memorable as 'landmarks' for her journey home.

● When you turn round to walk home, challenge your child to take you the correct way, passing familiar landmarks such as the blue house and the pretty cherry tree. Hopefully, your child will be able to point these out to you.

Taking it further

● Ask your child to shut her eyes and to tell you as much as she can remember about the environment immediately outside her house or school. Check her description with the actual environment.

LEARNING OPPORTUNITY
● To be aware of the usual sounds going on all around.

YOU WILL NEED
No special requirements.

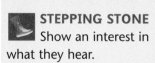

STEPPING STONE
Show an interest in what they hear.

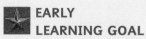

EARLY LEARNING GOAL
Creative development: Respond in a variety of ways to what they hear.

What's that sound?

Sharing the game

● This is a game to play with your child when he is playing outside in your garden or the park.

● Pretend that you are a visitor from outer space and you are feeling rather insecure in your new environment. Every sound is new to you and you are not sure whether you should be frightened by it or not.

● Ask your child to be your friend and to explain what all the different sounds are, and how you need to react when you hear them.

● Invite him to explain the various noises he can hear, for example, children laughing and talking, the roar of traffic, the sound of balls being kicked, babies crying, an ambulance or police siren, birds singing and so on.

● Are these all familiar sounds? Do any of them require any special action to be taken?

● Can your child hear anything he has not heard before? Encourage him to listen very carefully.

● Can you explain this new sound or do the two of you need to investigate it together?

Taking it further

● If your child plays somewhere he has never played before, is he likely to hear some of the same sounds he is used to? Is he likely to hear some new sounds?

SENSES COVERED
Smell.

LEARNING OPPORTUNITY
● To learn to recognise different smells.

YOU WILL NEED
Picnic food, for example, sausages, crisps, fish paste, marmite and banana sandwiches, jelly; teddies; paper plates; rug.

 STEPPING STONE
Show an interest in what they smell.

 EARLY LEARNING GOAL
Creative development: Respond in a variety of ways to what they smell.

Let's have a picnic

Sharing the game
● Suggest that your child organises a picnic for her teddies.
● Ask her to lay out a rug for the picnic and to put out the party food on to paper plates. Encourage her to smell the various foods.
● Does the smell of the food remind her of anything? Is it familiar? When might she have smelled this before?
● Can she remember seeing and smelling fish in the fresh produce area of the supermarket, in a fish and chip shop, or by the sea? Does the fish paste smell like this?
● Talk about other children's parties where she is likely to have had similar food. Has she smelled the marmite before, the crisps and the different-flavoured jelly?

● Has your child ever seen sausages cooking on a barbecue outside, perhaps as part of the food for a summer evening or for a bonfire party?
● Is any of this food part of her day-to-day diet and, therefore, very familiar to your child?
● Are there any new smells she does not recognise?

Taking it further
● Introduce a few, strong-smelling sweets (liquorice, peppermint and coffee creams), which might be new to your child. Encourage her to smell the new smells. Can she match these up with anything she has smelled before?

LEARNING OPPORTUNITY
● To learn about shapes and patterns.

YOU WILL NEED
Children's playground with a sand-pit; children's spade and rake; pebbles.

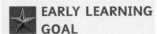
STEPPING STONE Show curiosity and observation by talking about shapes, how they are the same or why some are different.

EARLY LEARNING GOAL
Mathematical development: Talk about, recognise and recreate simple patterns.

Spot the shape

Sharing the game
● Remind your child what a square, a rectangle, a circle, an oval and a triangle look like and what their names are.

● Challenge your child to look out for different shapes while he is playing on the playground equipment. Can he see the rectangle shape of the see-saw, the circular tyres used for swings, the square windows in the playhouse, the triangular climbing frame and so on?

● Ask your child to create a picture in the sand-pit which is built up from lots of different shapes.

● Discuss patterns and what makes a simple pattern.

● Invite your child to make various patterns in the sand using the spade, rake and pebbles.

● Make a pattern for your child to copy and see if he can.

● Look out for other patterns in the playground or its surroundings, for example, the rungs on the ladder leading up to the slide, the bricks in the playground wall, the hopscotch markings and so on.

Taking it further
● Look out together for different-sized shapes, reminding your child that all shapes can be both big and small, and a number can also be fat or thin, and tall or short.

OUTDOOR FUN

SENSES COVERED
Sight, touch.

LEARNING OPPORTUNITY
● To experiment with paints.

YOU WILL NEED
Table with a wipeable surface that can go outside; poster paints in red, blue, yellow, white and black; brushes; water pots; child's apron; kitchen roll; cloths; paper.

STEPPING STONE
Explore what happens when they mix colours.

EARLY LEARNING GOAL
Creative development: Explore colour, texture, shape, form and space in two dimensions.

Magic painting

Sharing the game

● Take advantage of the sunshine to play a messy game outside.

● Help your child to put on the apron.

● Ask her to paint a picture on the table just using water. Note together how it disappears in a matter of minutes as the water evaporates in the sun.

● Now encourage her to experiment with the paints, mixing them with her fingers on the table to produce other colours. Note how the paints dry up and go hard if she leaves them undisturbed in the sun for any length of time. She must therefore work very quickly.

● Challenge her to produce as many different colours as she can. Which colour does she like best? Which colours has she seen in nature – on flowers or trees? Can she tell you how she made that pink or that bluey-green?

● Encourage her to make different patterns in the paint by using her fingers. She could swirl the paint round and round with one finger only, or use all five to squeeze the paint into a star shape. Invite your child to come up with other ideas. What does the paint feel like?

● When she is happy with her pattern, show her how to take a print of it by pressing a piece of kitchen roll down on to the paint and gently lifting it up again.

Taking it further

● Using some of the colours your child has mixed, encourage her to use brushes to paint a permanent picture on to paper.

Farms and zoos

Sharing the game

● Discuss the difference between domestic and wild animals, and the difference between farms and zoos.

● At a children's farm, your child is likely to be able to touch some of the animals as well as look at them, so encourage him to think about the fluffy feel of some fur, the rough, hairy feel of others and the velvety feel of muzzles and ears.

● Ask your child to look very carefully at the animals. What distinguishing features do they have? Look out for stripes, spots, long hair, strong legs, bushy tails, long ears, big horns and so on. Point out the great variety of browns, as well as greys, black and white.

● Challenge your child to recognise as many animals as he can. Give him the names of some of those he does not know.

● Listen to the sounds coming from the different parts of the farmyard or zoo. Can your child tell you what animals are around the corner? Which animals make the loudest, most obvious noise?

● What are the animals eating? Note different diets. Are any of them eating the same sort of food that we eat?

Taking it further

● After the visit, sing 'Old MacDonald' and encourage your child to join in with the animal sounds found both at the farm and at the zoo.

SENSES COVERED
Sight, hearing.

LEARNING OPPORTUNITY
● To learn a little about water birds.

YOU WILL NEED
A visit to a bird sanctuary or a pond with ducks, geese or swans.

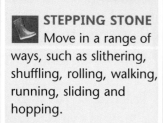

STEPPING STONE
Move in a range of ways, such as slithering, shuffling, rolling, walking, running, sliding and hopping.

EARLY LEARNING GOAL
Physical development: Move with confidence, imagination and in safety.

Quack, quack!

Sharing the game

● Talk about birds. Challenge your child to tell you some of the features which equip birds for the water (for example, feathers and webbed feet).

● During the visit, encourage your child to notice particularly the various ways birds move, both on the water and on the land.

● Listen to the sounds made by the birds' movements in the water, including the 'splash' as they land, the 'plop' as they do duck dives and the beating of the water as they take off from it.

● Following the visit, invite your child to pretend to be a bird.

● Slither along on the slippery mud.

● Roll from side to side as she washes her muddy feathers in the water.

● Shake the water off her oiled feathers.

● Shuffle along as she lands on the water.

● Slide as she tries to walk on the ice.

● Run along the water as she takes off from it.

● Curl up with her head tucked in behind her arm as she sleeps.

● Stand with her head down and bottom up as she eats weed from the bottom of the pond.

● Bob gently up and down as she goes above and below the surface of the water.

● Imitate the sound of some of the bird calls.

Taking it further

● Fill a basin with warm water. Ask your child to try pushing the water along with open fingers. Now try with closed fingers. Which works better? Make the link to webbed feet and how these propel birds through the water.

SENSES COVERED
Hearing.

LEARNING OPPORTUNITY
● To listen to the variety of sounds produced by the human voice, and to enjoy taking on roles when telling and acting out stories.

YOU WILL NEED
A visit to the library or theatre; picture books; dressing-up clothes.

 STEPPING STONE
Introduce a story line or narrative into their play.

EARLY LEARNING GOAL
Creative development: Use their imagination in role-play and stories.

Acting fun

Sharing the game

● Visit your local library for a storytime session. Encourage your child to listen carefully to the storyteller and notice how she changes her voice for the different characters and emotions that arise in the story.

● After a trip to the theatre, talk about the different actors and how they use their voices to portray the characters in the show.

● Invite your child to choose a well-known story to tell you. Encourage him to think about the different characters in the story and what they are doing before he begins. Ask him to put as much expression into the story as he can.

● From his telling, can you easily identify which are the 'good' characters and which the 'bad'? Offer suggestions as to how your child could change his voice more dramatically to make more of an impact. Discuss ideas together.

● With a group of his friends, encourage your child to act out a story for you. Give each child a role to play and help them to find appropriate costumes. Stress the importance of using suitable voices and also of moving in the way their characters would.

Taking it further

● Read your child a story, using no expression at all. Does he find the story interesting? Re-read it, using a number of different voices, some suitable and some not. How does your child feel about this reading? Read it once again, using appropriate expressions and voices. Which reading is the most enjoyable?

SENSES COVERED
Sight, hearing.

LEARNING OPPORTUNITY
● To understand warning messages given by our senses.

YOU WILL NEED
A visit to the seaside.

 STEPPING STONE
Express needs and feelings in appropriate ways.

 **EARLY LEARNING GOAL**
Personal, social and emotional development: Respond to significant experiences, showing a range of feelings when appropriate.

The seaside – look out!

Sharing the game
● When you arrive at the beach, play 'I spy' in order to notice what you normally see on a trip to the seaside, for example, a low tide with a sandy beach, a blue sky, lots of people around, birds gently pecking at the seaweed, dogs running around happily and so on.
● Discuss how your child's smiling face indicates her happiness.
● Consider what she would feel if she saw things changing, for

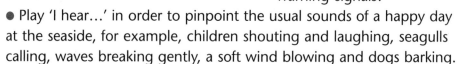

example, pathways between rocks disappearing under water, grey or black clouds approaching, lightning flashes in the sky, birds circling noisily overhead, dogs fighting and so on. How would the expression on her face change to show that she was unhappy, worried or frightened by these warning signals?

● Play 'I hear…' in order to pinpoint the usual sounds of a happy day at the seaside, for example, children shouting and laughing, seagulls calling, waves breaking gently, a soft wind blowing and dogs barking.
● Talk about how these sounds changing could be warning sounds indicating trouble ahead, such as children crying or screaming, seagulls screeching and squawking, waves crashing and roaring, howling wind or thunder, dogs growling and so on.
● If your child heard any of these things, what would she think, what would she feel and what would she do?

Taking it further
● Encourage your child to notice as many warning signals as she can when you are out and about, whether it's signs of the weather changing, people looking angry or sad, slippery surfaces or other natural hazards.
● Can she tell you about any sounds that act as warning signals, for example, loud bangs, screams, alarms and so on.

SENSES COVERED
Sight, hearing.

LEARNING OPPORTUNITY
● To learn how to protect themselves from the potential danger of traffic.

YOU WILL NEED
A long length of material; black sugar paper; white chalk.

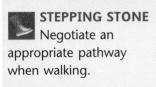

STEPPING STONE
Negotiate an appropriate pathway when walking.

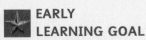

EARLY LEARNING GOAL
Physical development: Show awareness of space, of themselves and of others.

Danger!

Sharing the game

● Talk about busy roads and traffic, and the dangers it poses.

● Discuss the purpose of zebra and pelican crossings, explaining that zebra crossings are identified by orange beacons, whereas pelican crossings are situated at traffic lights. Traffic should stop when they see

someone waiting at a zebra crossing, making it safe for them to cross. At pelican crossings, traffic is controlled by traffic lights and a green light showing a walking man will indicate when it is safe for pedestrians to cross.

● Explain, however, that we should always use the Green Cross Code every time we cross a road.

● Encourage your child to become totally familiar with this routine by playing the following game.

● Unroll the material and lay it out on the floor as a pretend road.

● Draw white stripes on the black paper to make a 'zebra crossing' and place this across the 'road'.

● Hold your child's hand and stand with him at the side of the road.

● Go through the 'Stop, look and listen' routine, making sure that your child looks right, then left, then right again and listens carefully for approaching traffic (make car noises as appropriate), before walking straight across the road, while still holding your hand.

Taking it further

● Encourage your child to ride his tricycle in the park or playground. Point out how difficult it is for him to stop quickly once he has gathered speed. This is why it is so important not to get in the way of moving traffic.

SENSES COVERED
Hearing, sight, smell.

LEARNING OPPORTUNITY
● To learn when it is necessary to take immediate action to avert disaster.

YOU WILL NEED
Two toy telephones; emergency service dressing-up clothes.

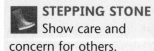

THINK FIRST!
Take care not to frighten your child unduly, while still emphasising the need for action.

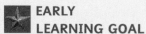

STEPPING STONE
Show care and concern for others.

EARLY LEARNING GOAL
Personal, social and emotional development: Consider the consequences of their actions for themselves and others.

Emergency!

Sharing the game

● Discuss what the word 'emergency' means and how police, ambulance workers and firefighters are there to help. Explain the difference between a real emergency and a situation where your child is feeling angry or mildly hurt. Read her a story, such as 'Peter and the Wolf', to emphasise the importance of reserving loud screams and calls for help for emergencies only, so that she is not ignored when she really needs help.

● Talk about how loud screams, alarms and sirens can be very helpful in alerting other people around you and, therefore, in getting help quickly.

● Our senses of sight and smell can also be very useful in alerting us to real dangers, such as smoke or fire coming from a burning building.

● Explain that in an emergency, you can make a phone call to the emergency services to tell them what has happened and to ask for the appropriate services to be sent out.

● Ask your child to pretend she is an ambulance worker, firefighter or policeman responding to such a call from you. Use the toy phones. She should listen carefully to what you are saying, agree whether the fire, police or ambulance service is required, take your address and tell you that she will be there very soon.

Taking it further

● Try to visit a fire station. Note the loud alarm bells and sirens, and point out the flashing lights and open doors on the fire engines. In an emergency, everyone is alerted quickly.

ROLE-PLAY

Young children can learn an enormous amount through play, and setting up simple role-play situations is an excellent way of stimulating this constructive play. A small corner of the room, together with a few simple props, is all that is required to create lots of different scenarios that will provide hours of imaginative fun for children.

The games in this chapter are linked to various role-play situations and they all focus on using one or more of the senses as children play. Many of the games also introduce the children to other countries and cultures from around the world, including their festivals, traditions, clothes, food and music.

ROLE-PLAY

Almost all children enjoy dressing up and indulging in pretend play. At the age of three, their imaginary play will mostly revolve around familiar situations in the home environment, for example, cooking in the kitchen, putting babies to bed and talking on the telephone. At the age of four, they will start to introduce other elements into their play, based on their growing experiences, such as shopping for clothes and food, going to the doctor and eating in cafés. By the time they reach five years old, they will be able to indulge in imaginary play, based on a whole range of different scenarios made familiar through story books, television and visits to the theatre, for example, being a king or queen in their castle, flying in a rocket, exploring the jungle and so on.

How you can help

● Try to have an area in your room where your child can indulge in imaginary play.
● Provide simple props to create a variety of different scenarios, for example, small tables and chairs, plastic crockery, cutlery and beakers, dolls, cots, bedding, pretend food and food packets, a doctor's kit and so on.
● Make sure you have a selection of dressing-up clothes available so that your child can assume different roles.
● Encourage him to make some of the props which will help to create the right atmosphere for any particular setting, for example, flowers and greenery, necklaces, gold coins and so on.

● Be prepared to join in with his imaginary scenarios and encourage him to invite his friends to play.
● Introduce new ideas for play, so that your child's creative instincts are stretched to the full and his capacity for constructive play is never exhausted.

USING THE SENSES DURING PLAY

The games in this chapter involve using one or more of the senses as children play. In reality, almost all imaginary play situations use the senses in some way or another. Children, however, will not necessarily make the most of these opportunities for using their senses unless they are told what to look out for, what to listen for, what to feel, what to smell and, on occasion, what to taste.

How you can help

● As you prepare the play area together, take every opportunity to encourage your child to use her senses.

● Ask her what she can see, tell her to examine things very carefully and challenge her to notice details, such as different shades of colour.

● Encourage your child to be aware of new sounds and to describe what she can hear.

● Ask her about the texture and feel of different objects and materials. How would she describe them?

● As your child plays, continue to point out things for her to notice with her senses, including smells and tastes.

APPRECIATING OTHER CULTURES DURING PLAY

Learning about and appreciating other cultures and countries is important for children. They have to understand about other people's ways of life in order to be sensitive to their needs. Introducing this learning in a role-play situation makes it much more real and much easier for young children to understand.

How you can help

● Look at maps and a globe together to discover where other countries are in relation to where you live.

● Discuss the geographical features of some of the other countries. How are they different?

● Encourage your child to learn as much as he can about other cultures from his friends and contemporaries at school.

● Discuss festivals that you celebrate together. Do you wear special clothes, eat special food, give each other presents or decorate the house in some way?

● Learn together about other festivals around the world and how they are celebrated.

● Look at picture books together to see how housing and clothing differs in some other parts of the world.

● Give your child a varied diet so that he gets used to lots of different food (for example, fruit and vegetables from all over the world) and to lots of different ways of preparing it (for example, roast dinners, curries, pasta and stews).

● Play a variety of different music for your child to listen to, so that he becomes familiar with the sound of music from other parts of the world.

MAKING FRIENDS DURING PLAY

Playing together is a very positive way for children to develop friendships. Role-play involves children in co-operative play, where everyone is included and children learn how to give, take and share. Three-year-olds find this initial sharing and negotiating quite difficult. Many are used to having their own way and putting themselves first. However, as they grow older, at the ages of four and, even more so, at five, children learn how to share and play happily together, taking turns and exchanging roles, as they understand the benefits of doing so and see how much fun they can have when they co-operate together.

How you can help

● Encourage your child to always have a go at everything, even things she initially finds hard.

● Make sure she understands how important it is to be kind to others, to include them in her play and to share.

● Invite classmates to your house and accept invitations for your child to visit friends away from home.

● Join in your child's play to encourage her to develop and continue it.

● Include your child in discussions and let her speak for herself when asked questions.

● Encourage her to be excited by new opportunities and experiences.

SENSES COVERED
Sight, touch.

LEARNING OPPORTUNITY
● To learn a little about Divali.

YOU WILL NEED
A corner of your room set up as a playhouse; modelling clay; yellow tissue paper; threading beads; scissors; sugar paper; finger-paints; masking tape; pictures of rangoli patterns (if possible).

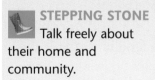

STEPPING STONE
Talk freely about their home and community.

EARLY LEARNING GOAL
Personal, social and emotional development: Have a developing respect for their own cultures and beliefs and those of other people.

Ready for Divali

Sharing the game
● Tell your child about the Hindu festival of Divali, held in November, marking the Hindu New Year.
● Explain how houses are decorated with rangoli patterns and lit up with strings of lights and oil lamps.
● Invite your child to help you make small Divali lamps to decorate your 'house'.
● Show him how to mould modelling clay into the shape of a lamp. See if he can make a series of lamps from large to small.
● Help him to cut out flames from the tissue paper and fix these into the clay to finish off the lamps.
● Ask your child to make strings of beads for lights, copying a pattern you have given him.
● Look very carefully at pictures of rangoli patterns and encourage your child to copy some of these patterns on to sugar paper, using finger-paints. Make sure he enjoys the 'gooey' feel of the paints.
● Help him to tape the rangoli patterns on to the floor in front of your playhouse.
● Fix the strings of beads to the walls of the house and place the lamps inside.
● Encourage your child to enjoy the festive feel of Divali.

Taking it further
● Divali is also marked with fireworks. Ask your child to close his eyes and imagine that he is watching a firework display. Ask him to describe what he can see and hear.
● Talk about the dangers of fireworks.

SENSES COVERED
Sight, touch.

LEARNING OPPORTUNITY
● To learn a little about clothing worn in other parts of the world.

YOU WILL NEED
Pictures of women in traditional costume from around the world or costume dolls; a collection of fabric pieces including net and lace (curtains are a good source); skirts; dresses; hats; table; coat-hangers and hooks; boxes; mirror; a globe.

 STEPPING STONE
Use available resources to create props to support role-play.

EARLY LEARNING GOAL
Creative development: Use their imagination in design and role-play.

Where am I from?

Sharing the game

● Show the pictures or dolls to your child and look at a globe to locate the various countries they come from.

● Talk about the different kinds of traditional costume.

● Invite your child to set up a clothes shop in a corner of your room. Hang up the dresses and skirts, and display the hats on a table.

● Ask your child to put the fabric pieces into several different boxes, sorting them by texture and weight.

● Encourage her to think about which fabric would be suitable for certain items of clothing, for example, saris, kimonos, head-dresses, veils and so on.

● Include a mirror somewhere in the shop.

● Assume the role of shopkeeper and invite your child to come to the shop to buy an outfit. Ask her to choose the type of clothing she wants from the pictures.

● If necessary, help her to wrap the fabric around herself to make a costume which looks like one from a picture or doll.

● When dressed, can she tell you where she is from?

Taking it further

● Help your child to make other accessories, such as jewellery, to complement the outfits.

● Fold thin card and decorate to make fans.

● Stick decorations on to an old umbrella to make a parasol.

SENSES COVERED
Hearing.

LEARNING OPPORTUNITY
● To appreciate different kinds of music from all over the world.

YOU WILL NEED
A selection of musical instruments – string, wind and percussion; small tables; tape recorder or CD player; examples of music from around the world (for example, Scottish bagpipes, Spanish guitar, Caribbean steel drums, Indian sitars, Greek bouzoukis, Italian mandolins, Chinese zithers, Romanian panpipes, Irish flutes).

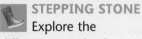 **STEPPING STONE**
Explore the different sounds of instruments.

 EARLY LEARNING GOAL
Creative development: Recognise sound patterns and match movements to music.

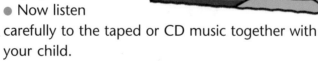

Hear the music

Sharing the game

● Help your child to create a music shop in a corner of your room. Spread out any instruments that you have available on the tables and set up the tape recorder or CD player.

● Help him to make labels identifying and pricing each of the instruments.

● Talk about the different types of musical instruments (percussion, string and wind). Explain how each one is played.

● Ask your child to sort your selection of instruments by type and encourage him to have a go at playing them. Which does he find easiest to play?

● Now listen carefully to the taped or CD music together with your child.

● Ask him to think about the music in a number of different ways.

● Does he like it?

● Can he tell what type of instrument is playing?

● Is it happy or sad?

● Is it loud or soft?

● How would he describe the sound it makes?

● What does the music suggest to him?

● Invite him to make up dances for the different kinds of music.

Taking it further

● Suggest your child invites a few of his friends to his shop to try out some of the instruments. Can they make up their own music together or accompany some of the taped music you have collected?

LEARNING OPPORTUNITY
● To learn about other parts of the world.

YOU WILL NEED
A map of the world; travel brochures; pictures of key tourist sites; postcards from different countries; table and chairs; masking tape.

 STEPPING STONE Show an interest in the world in which they live.

EARLY LEARNING GOAL
Knowledge and understanding of the world: Observe, find out about and identify features in the natural world.

Holiday time

Sharing the game

● Discuss going on holiday and the role of travel agents.

● Invite your child to help you set up a travel-agents shop in a corner of your room.

● Think together about the different types of holiday that people can take – in cities, at the seaside, in the country and so on.

● Ask your child how people get to where they want to go. Can she tell you about different means of transport?

● Arrange the travel agents so that there is a set of table and chairs, and different brochures to look at.

● Fix a large world map to the wall and help your child to stick the postcards in the correct place on the map, using masking tape.

● Hang up some of the pictures as well. Challenge your child to tell you whether any of these match one of the postcards.

● Examine the travel brochures together. Where would your child like to go? Can she tell you why?

● Find the destination on the map. Look at the route from where you live to where you want to holiday. Will you have to cross any blue areas on the map? Explain that these are seas and oceans. Can your child tell you how you might cross these?

Taking it further

● Challenge your child to find unfamiliar sights in the travel brochures which are characteristic of particular countries. These might be unusual flowers and trees, animals and birds, different buildings, lots of snow and so on.

LEARNING
OPPORTUNITY
● To learn about Italian
food.

YOU WILL NEED
Paper plates; brightly-
coloured paper; scissors;
PVA glue; coloured
modelling clay; dry pasta
of several varieties; plastic
plates and cutlery;
takeaway pizza menus;
table; chairs; table-cloth.

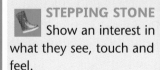 **STEPPING STONE**
Show an interest in
what they see, touch and
feel.

 **EARLY LEARNING
GOAL**
Creative development:
Express and
communicate their ideas
by using a widening
range of materials,
imaginative and role-
play.

I love pizza!

Sharing the game

● Invite your child to set up a small Italian restaurant in a corner of
your room.

● Examine the several
varieties of pasta and
discuss the wide range
of toppings available
for pizza.

● Help your child to
set up the corner as
his restaurant,
covering the table
with the cloth and
laying it with the
plates and cutlery.

● Place the menus on the table.

● Invite your child to make several sample dishes for the restaurant.
Help him to cut out and stick the coloured paper on to the paper
plates, using different colours for different ingredients. If the pizza has
a tomato base, cut a large circle of red to fit on to the paper plate. For
pepperoni, use small circles of brown paper; for olives, use circles of
green and so on.

● Assemble pasta dishes in a similar way but use small pieces of
coloured modelling clay instead of the paper for the different
ingredients (for example, tomato, bacon and peas).

● Encourage your child to think about the smell and taste of each
dish as he is assembling it.

● Be a customer in the restaurant, order a pizza or pasta dish and
challenge your child to make it up especially for you.

Taking it further

● Cook some dried pasta in plenty of water for 15 minutes or so, and
let it cool down. Encourage your child to notice how the hard, sharp,
dry pasta turns soft and sticky when cooked. Always supervise your
child carefully in the kitchen and point out the dangers of hot rings,
utensils and very hot food.

ROLE-PLAY

SENSES COVERED
Touch.

LEARNING OPPORTUNITY
● To be aware of different fur and feathers.

YOU WILL NEED
A selection of soft toys and other animal toys; feathers – both down and wing; samples of fabric – fake fur, velvet and so on; cardboard boxes (for cages); pencils and paper (for labels); books about pets with 'feely' pictures.

 STEPPING STONE
Show an interest in what they touch and feel.

EARLY LEARNING GOAL
Creative development: Respond in a variety of ways to what they touch and feel.

All kinds of pets

Sharing the game
● Talk about the different animals and birds that children have as pets, and look at the 'feely' books and material samples together.
● Encourage your child to talk about each one and to tell you about the textures of their fur, skin, shell or scales.

● Many pets have fur, like your child's soft toys. Does all fur feel the same? Invite your child to feel all her soft toys. Compare the feel of matted, short, wiry fur with that which is long and fluffy. Can she guess which of her toys will feel the softest?
● Touch whiskers and noses. What do they feel like?
● Feel the pads on the toys' feet? Are they harder or softer than the fur? Can your child suggest why?
● Invite her to set up a corner of your room as a pet shop. Let her put the soft toys into 'cages' and display them with their names and prices.
● Encourage her to ask her friends to come and see the pets in the shop.

● Compare the feel of the different bird feathers. Note how a wing feather is much stronger than a down feather. Which would make the fluffier pillow? Can your child explain why the wing feathers need to be strong?

Taking it further
● Invite your child to compare different pet food. Feel the different texture of dried, tinned and fresh food, and note which has the strongest smell. (Wash hands carefully afterwards.)

SENSES COVERED
Smell, taste.

LEARNING OPPORTUNITY
● To do some simple cooking.

YOU WILL NEED
125g butter; 125g soft brown sugar; two eggs; 125g self-raising flour; 60g raisins; glacé cherries; one pear, peeled and finely chopped; mixing bowl; wooden spoon; bun tin; plate; table; money; aprons.

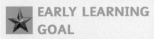

THINK FIRST!
Make sure your child washes his hands carefully before touching any food.

STEPPING STONE
Show an interest in number problems.

EARLY LEARNING GOAL
Mathematical development: In practical activities begin to use the vocabulary involved in adding and subtracting.

The bakery

Sharing the game
● Invite your child to help you make some raisin-pear cakes for the baker's shop. Put aprons on.
● Help him to beat the butter and sugar together until creamy.
● Let him crack the eggs and beat them carefully, one at a time, into the mixture.
● Help your child to fold in the flour.
● Let him add the raisins and chopped pear.
● Encourage him to give the mixture a final good mix before spooning it into the greased bun tin.
● Let him put a glacé cherry on the top of each cake.
● Bake for 7–10 minutes at 350°F/180°C/Gas Mark 4.
● Make sure your child notices the smell of the cakes as they cook.
● Ask him to set up a baker's shop in the corner of your room.
● When the cakes are cool, put them on a plate on the table.
● Invite him to come to the shop with his money and remove the cakes, one by one, using the rhyme 'Six raisin-pear cakes in the baker's shop' on page 128.

Taking it further
● Let your child sample the cakes. Do they taste as he expects them to?
● Imagine the taste of other items sold in a baker's shops (bread, rolls, sausage rolls, cakes and so on).
● Can he imagine the lovely smells?

LEARNING OPPORTUNITY
● To be aware of the environment in a tropical rainforest.

YOU WILL NEED
Books showing the vegetation found in tropical rainforests; paper; card; fabric in various shades of green, of various weights and with a variety of surfaces, including shiny ones (for example, hessian, PVC, tweed, velvet and net); masking tape; thick string; scissors.

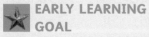 **STEPPING STONE**
Begin to use talk to pretend imaginary situations.

EARLY LEARNING GOAL
Communication, language and literacy: Use language to imagine and recreate roles and experiences.

So many plants!

Sharing the game

● Look carefully at the rainforest pictures, encouraging your child to notice as many different leaves as she can.

● As well as the shape and size of the leaf, invite her to notice any other differences, such as colour and texture. Also look out for holes or indents in the leaves.

● Challenge your child to reproduce as many of the tropical plants as she can by choosing the most suitable paper or material to work with.

● Help her to cut the paper and fabric into the correct shape and size for the leaves.

● Fix lengths of string to the ceiling in a corner of your room and help your child to attach her leaves to these, in order to produce very thick vegetation.

● Encourage your child to talk about how she feels as she fights her way through this thick vegetation. Does it seem dark? What can she see? What does she touch as she walks along? What are her feelings as she sets foot in this strange environment?

● Can she make up a story set in this environment?

Taking it further

● Make spiders by twisting black pipe-cleaners together.
● Make small butterflies by attaching coloured tissue paper into yellow pipe-cleaners.
● Attach both of these to the thick vegetation to provide more textures to feel.

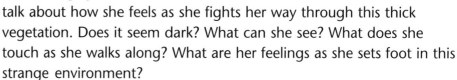

LEARNING OPPORTUNITY
● To explore a variety of fruit and vegetables.

YOU WILL NEED
A selection of fruit and vegetables from around the world; small tables; paper plates and baskets; potato peeler and knife (for adult use only).

STEPPING STONE
Examine objects to find out more about them.

EARLY LEARNING GOAL
Knowledge and understanding of the world: Investigate objects by using all of their senses as appropriate.

So good for you!

Sharing the game

● Encourage your child to examine all the fruit and vegetables carefully, noting the colour, shape, texture and smell of each whole fruit or vegetable.

● Suggest that he sets up his own greengrocer's shop in a corner of your room.

● Ask him to display the different fruit and vegetables on the tables, using the baskets and plates.

● Invite your child to come to the shop to buy some of the more unusual fruit and vegetables. Encourage him to choose some which have a different appearance when they are peeled or chopped up, for example, passion fruit, kiwi fruits, pineapples, melons, lychees, aubergines, courgettes, sweet potatoes and so on.

● Using the produce he has bought, challenge him to guess whether the colour of the fruit or vegetable will alter when it is peeled. What colour does your child think the inside might be?

● Cut open or peel the fruit for your child to see. Is the texture inside very different from the outside? Can he see any seeds or stones? How has the smell changed, or is it still the same?

● Finally, let your child taste some of the fruit. Does he like it? How would he describe the taste?

Taking it further

● Make a fruit salad together, using lots of different fruits.

● Enjoy the vibrant mix of colours and the wonderful fruity smell.

● Let your child get the juice from an orange and a lemon using a squeezer, to add to the salad.

● Let him taste the final result.

SENSES COVERED
Hearing, sight.

LEARNING OPPORTUNITY
● To hear another language being spoken and to understand a few French words.

YOU WILL NEED
Small tables; a French baguette; empty packaging from French food; tape or CD of French songs with plenty of repeated refrains; tape recorder or CD player.

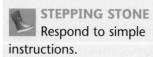 **STEPPING STONE**
Respond to simple instructions.

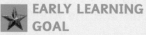 **EARLY LEARNING GOAL**
Communication, language and literacy: Enjoy listening to and using spoken language, and readily turn to it in their play and learning.

Shopping in France

Sharing the game

● Discuss the fact that many people in other countries speak different languages. There are lots of different languages in the world.

● Listen to the tape or CD, and encourage your child to identify and join in with the repeated refrains in the songs.

● Explain to your child that she is going to learn a little about the French language, by setting up a French shop in a corner of your room.

● Give her the baguette and the empty French food packages, and ask her to arrange these on the small tables.

● Tell your child a number of French words, for example, 'pain' for bread, 'fromage' for cheese, 's'il vous plait' for please and 'merci' for thank you. Practise saying these with her.

● Encourage her to watch and listen very carefully as you show her how she should ask for bread or cheese in a French shop. 'Du pain, s'il vous plait' or, 'Du fromage, s'il vous plait' and then, 'Merci'.

● Now invite her to come and buy at the shop. Encourage her to try to ask you (the shopkeeper) by herself, but offer help if necessary, encouraging her to say the words with you.

Taking it further

● Let your child enjoy the crunchy taste of a fresh French baguette.
● Introduce her to the smell of some ripe French cheeses and notice the strong odours.

Decorating

Sharing the game

● Your child is going to pretend to be a painter and decorator who will come to your house with examples of everything he can do. You can then choose the colours and effects you want in your home.
● Set up a working area for your child with the table, the poster paint and the painting tools.
● To start with, suggest that he should make a colour chart.

● Ask him to brush small samples of poster paint on to sugar paper to show his range of colours. He will need to mix some of the paints in the small trays so that he can offer you at least 20 different colours.
● Next, he needs to make samples of his sponging and rag-rolling so that you can see what these will look like.
● Encourage your child to scrumple the rag into a tight ball and then dip it into a tray of fairly watery paint, before rolling it on to the sugar paper to create a mottled effect.
● Next, invite him to dip the sponge into the watery paint, before squeezing it dry and dabbing it over the paper to produce a very different effect.
● Let all the pieces dry and then ask your child to come to you with his samples, so that you can make a decision about what you would like in your home.

Taking it further

● Encourage your child to experiment with different effects, for example, a thick layer of paint brushed or combed over.
● Ask him to try building up layers of sponging in different colours for a multi-coloured effect.

SENSES COVERED
Hearing, sight, touch.

LEARNING OPPORTUNITY
● To respond to instructions, to learn to look carefully and to hold on tightly when exploring challenging equipment.

YOU WILL NEED
An obstacle course created from several pieces of play equipment (for example, a tunnel, climbing frame, bench and mat) in a corner of your room or access to a playground or soft-play centre.

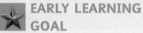 **STEPPING STONE** Mount stairs, steps or climbing equipment using alternate feet.

EARLY LEARNING GOAL
Physical development: Travel around, under, over and through balancing and climbing equipment.

Let's get fit!

Sharing the game

● Tell your child that you are going to direct her through the obstacle course as a keep-fit exercise. You will tell her what to do.

● Explain that she must listen very carefully and respond to what you ask her to do, for example, crawl through the tunnel, climb up the climbing frame, slide down the slide, walk along the bench and roll sideways across the mat.

● Challenge your child to complete the course in the correct order and in the correct way, without slipping or falling.

● Point out that, in order to do this, she will need to hold on to the equipment and balance very carefully.

● Make sure she realises that it is better to go slowly, rather than to risk falling when she is rushing.

● Encourage her to use her hands to feel her way through the tunnel, to hold on tightly to the frame as she climbs up, to sit upright on the slide, to look extremely carefully at the bench as she walks along it and to tuck in her arms and legs beside her body as she rolls along.

Taking it further

● Play 'Simon says', telling your child what actions to perform. Your child must only respond if 'Simon' says she must do something. Otherwise, she should remain still. Encourage her to listen very carefully so that she is not caught out.

● Share the nursery rhyme 'This is the way the ladies ride' on page 128.

CHAPTER 8

It is important for children to be aware of and to understand physical disabilities and sensory impairments in other people. It will help them to realise what an important part the senses play in all of our lives. It will give them lots of reassurance that children are able to cope remarkably well with everyday tasks and activities, despite experiencing these difficulties. It will also help them to appreciate the importance of including everyone in their play, so that no one feels left out or isolated.

The games in this chapter concentrate mainly on various sensory disabilities and how people can overcome them.

FRIENDS TOGETHER

How you can help
● Talk about the different disabilities that sometimes affect children and adults, for example, hearing impairment, visual impairment, and other sensory and physical impairments.
● As you go out and about, show your child any special provisions for those with these disabilities, for example, white sticks, guide dogs, flashing warning lights, people using sign language, ramps for wheelchairs, disabled toilets and wide access doors.
● Explain to your child the need for these special provisions and the purpose of them.
● Encourage him to ask questions to increase his understanding.

RAISING AWARENESS
Most young children will be very aware of the different sights and sounds around them, but they may not appreciate the full significance of those sights and sounds and how they help other people. For example, young children may not realise how important all the everyday sounds are to people who cannot see.

It will depend on each child's own particular circumstances, but some children may not come across any form of disability until they are a little older. Until they do meet someone with a difficulty, they will not be able to fully appreciate what this disability means in terms of everyday life.

Children who have not seen or experienced physical disability or sensory deprivation for themselves, will need to have these difficulties explained to them in order to understand the important role our senses play in everyday life.

experienced by people, concentrating especially on the two most common ones – hearing and visual deprivation.

● Encourage her to imagine what it must be like when you cannot hear anything. We live in such a noisy world, it is very hard to come across total silence, but endeavour to create this around your child for a short while and ask her to tell you what she thinks about when she can hear nothing.

● Encourage her to close her eyes and imagine what it must be like not to be able to see anything. Again, what does she think about?

● Invite her to put on a pair of thick gardening gloves and then to try to stroke her favourite teddy. What does it feel like not having that sense of touch?

UNDERSTANDING OTHERS' NEEDS

Learning to get on with others, to be inclusive and tolerant are key skills to have. It is essential for children to learn how to be sensitive to the needs of others and to develop responsibility towards them, if they are going to get on with them.

Children become tolerant and will include others if they can understand how differences enrich life and make everything more fun.

How you can help

● Encourage your child to be aware of his own feelings and those of others. Help him to express his emotions by reflecting how you think he is

feeling, for example, 'I can see you are frustrated by not being able to put that together – can I help you?'.

● As he plays, make sure he listens to others and watches how they react in certain situations, so that he learns more about them.

● Encourage your child to be tolerant by explaining why everyone is important and has their own contribution to make.

● Discuss how everyone is different and why these differences make life much more interesting.

● Show him how much extra fun he can have when other children are included in his play.

● Encourage him to show responsibility for his own actions.

● Be a good role-model and show your child how to be friendly and helpful to other people.

SENSORY DEPRIVATION

The various disabilities caused by a loss of one or more of the senses are known as sensory deprivation. Some people are born with these impairments, while others develop them as a result of accident or illness. It is difficult to appreciate what people, who have never been able to see, imagine when they are given a verbal description. However, verbal descriptions are very helpful in giving someone who has lost their sight at a later stage, a very clear picture in their mind. Equally, someone who is totally deaf at birth will never know the sound of birds singing, whereas it is possible to 'hear' that sound in their imagination if the sense is lost at a later stage.

How you can help

● Talk to your child about the various sensory impairments that can be

SENSES COVERED
Touch.

LEARNING OPPORTUNITY
● To explain a little about the needs of people with visual impairment.

YOU WILL NEED
A book in Braille; computer keyboard; books about guide dogs.

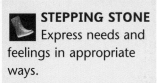 **STEPPING STONE** Express needs and feelings in appropriate ways.

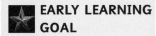 **EARLY LEARNING GOAL**
Personal, social and emotional development: Have a developing awareness of their own needs, views and feelings and be sensitive to the needs, views and feelings of others.

When I can't see

Sharing the game
● Talk to your child about visual impairment and what it means to the person who cannot see.
● Discuss how a person who is visually impaired has to 'see' by other means, for example, touch.
● Explain to your child how Braille works. Tell him that the raised bumps represent letters and words, which can then be identified by touching them with your fingers.

● Pass your child the Braille book and let him feel the bumps for himself.
● Explain that this is how people who are fully or partially visually impaired are able to read.
● Let your child use a computer keyboard and show him how people who touch-type place their hands. Explain how this helps them to remember where the various letters are and enables them to write without having to look at the keyboard. They can feel when they have got it right.
● Look at the pictures of guide dogs and explain their role. These dogs 'see' for their owner who cannot use his or her own eyes. They lead their owner safely around.

Taking it further
● Invite your child to try being a careful guide dog. Close your eyes and ask him to hold your hand while he leads you carefully around the room. Do you feel safe with your child?
● Suggest that your child tries to type without looking. Show him where the letters for his name are on the keyboard. Let him type it lots of times while looking at the keys. When he feels confident that he knows where the letters are, ask him to look straight ahead and to try typing without looking.
● Look at the Royal National Institute for the Blind (RNIB) website for more information www.rnib.org.uk

Listen instead of looking

Sharing the game

● Talk to your child about children with visual impairment and how it changes their everyday enjoyment of life.

● Discuss what these children might miss seeing.

● It is not possible for some visually-impaired children to watch television or to see pictures in books, but it is possible for them to get equal enjoyment from listening to the radio, tapes or to people reading books to them, or from playing an instrument. Spend some time looking at and listening to these various items (optional).

● Instead of their eyes seeing pictures, when they listen to stories their imaginations get used to creating vivid images in their brains.

● Read a story to your child but do not show her any of the pictures. Every so often, ask her to describe the picture she is 'seeing' as she listens. Look to see whether her picture matches the one in the book. If not, which does she like best?

● Often people who cannot see develop other senses which are very acute and they can hear subtle changes in sounds.

● Visually-impaired children can still enjoy music and all the wonderful sounds of nature.

● They can listen to others describing sights to them and can build up their own detailed pictures.

Taking it further

● Describe a favourite item of clothing. Challenge your child to draw a picture of it, just by listening to your description.

● See if your child can hear the difference between two very similar sounds when she shuts her eyes and concentrates completely on listening. If she cannot hear a difference, ask her to try again.

 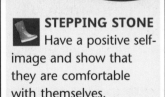

STEPPING STONE
Have a positive self-image and show that they are comfortable with themselves.

EARLY LEARNING GOAL
Personal, social and emotional development:
Understand that people have different needs that need to be treated with respect.

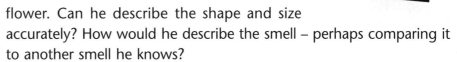

SENSES COVERED
Smell, touch.

LEARNING OPPORTUNITY
● To be able to get pleasure from using the senses of smell and touch when unable to see.

YOU WILL NEED
A selection of heavily-scented flowers (for example, stocks, roses, freesias, lavender, lilac); strong-smelling food.

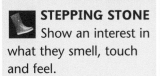

STEPPING STONE
Show an interest in what they smell, touch and feel.

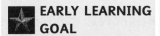

EARLY LEARNING GOAL
Creative development: Respond in a variety of ways to what they smell, touch and feel.

Smell and touch to 'see'

Sharing the game
● Discuss visual impairment and how it is possible to still gain pleasure from some of the wonderful things around us by using senses other than sight.
● Children who cannot see may be unable to enjoy the colours and pretty look of flowers, but they can still enjoy the smell of them and also explore their shape, size and texture by touching and feeling them.
● Ask your child to shut his eyes, pretending he cannot see and hand him each flower in turn.
● Encourage him to explore it thoroughly, using his senses of smell and touch.
● Ask him to tell you all he can about the flower. Can he describe the shape and size accurately? How would he describe the smell – perhaps comparing it to another smell he knows?
● Again, with his eyes shut, encourage your child to enjoy various foods by their smell, when you put the foods near him.
● Point out that the enjoyable smell is not diminished by being unable to see the food.

Taking it further
● When your child has finished telling you about each flower, compare his description with the actual look of the flower.
● Can your child tell you which foods he is smelling?
● Share the rhyme 'Summer breeze' on page 128.

LEARNING OPPORTUNITY
● To develop an acute sense of taste and touch.

YOU WILL NEED
A complete meal with a mixture of tastes and textures both in the savoury dish (for example, chicken and vegetable casserole) and in the sweet (for example, fruit crumble and ice-cream).

 STEPPING STONE
Show awareness of own needs with regard to eating.

EARLY LEARNING GOAL
Physical development: Recognise the importance of keeping healthy and those things which contribute to this.

Taste and texture

Sharing the game
● Discuss the importance of eating sensibly in order to keep healthy.
● Talk about cooking meals and explain to your child that most dishes contain several ingredients mixed together.
● Usually, we can see many of these ingredients when we look at our food before we eat it.
● However, for children who are visually impaired this may not be possible, so they have to develop other ways of working out what makes their food taste so good.

● Initially, their sense of taste tells them whether or not they like their food. However, this can be developed to give them more detailed information as to the make-up of their meal.
● Ask your child to close her eyes while you feed her some of her meal.
● Can she identify any of the separate tastes and textures of the food, for example, carrots, chicken, onions, potatoes, peas, cabbage and so on?

● With the pudding, encourage her to notice the contrasting textures and temperatures of her food.

Taking it further
● Challenge your child to notice certain ingredients in different dishes, particularly by their taste. What ingredients appear again and again in food she especially likes?
● Tell your child the ingredients that are in a particular dish. Does she think she will like it? Encourage her to taste it. Was she right?

SENSES COVERED
Sight.

LEARNING OPPORTUNITY
● To develop good imaginative skills when unable to hear.

YOU WILL NEED
A video of a children's story that your child does not know, told with lots of pictures.

 STEPPING STONE
Begin to use talk instead of action to rehearse, re-order and reflect on past experience, linking significant events from stories, paying attention to sequence and how events lead into one another.

EARLY LEARNING GOAL
Communication, language and literacy: Use language to imagine and recreate roles and experiences.

When I can't hear

Sharing the game
● Discuss children who are hearing impaired. What does this mean in terms of their enjoyment?
● Explain that they may not be able to enjoy listening to stories being read to them or told to them.
● On the other hand, if they are able to see, they can enjoy looking at the pictures which accompany stories and they can look at television or video pictures.
● As they are unable to hear the story, it is important for them to be able to make up their own stories to go with the pictures. They need to imagine what is going on.
● Explain that you are going to ask your child to imagine that he cannot hear the video and can only see the pictures.
● You are going to ask him to use his imagination to tell you the story which is being told on the video.
● Show him the video all the way through, with the sound turned off.
● Then start it again and encourage your child to use his imagination to make up the story, developing it as the pictures are shown on the screen.

Taking it further
● When your child has had a go at telling the story from the pictures, watch the video with the sound turned up.
● How did his own version compare with the video version?

Learning to mime

Sharing the game

● Discuss with your child how someone with a hearing impairment might feel isolated.

● Explain that you want your child to imagine that she is trying to include her hearing-impaired friend (you) in her play, so that she does not feel left out.

● Encourage her to come up with ways of telling her friend (you) what she is doing and how she would like her friend to be involved.

● Your child must bear in mind that her friend is relying on her sense of sight to understand what is being said to her.

● Wait for your child's suggestions, but be ready to help with ideas if necessary.

● How might she tell her friend that she wants her to come? (Direct eye contact and a beckoning signal with her arm.)

● How might she tell her that they are going to go on an imaginary car journey? (A driving-wheel motion with her hands.)

● How might she tell her that other children are going to be involved in the play? (Pointing directly at the other children and then pointing to the two of you.)

● How would she ask her friend if she wanted a drink? (Raising her thumb and forefinger together to her mouth with a questioning look in her eyes.)

● Can she think of other ways of using miming actions?

Taking it further

● Explain to your child that there are several recognised sign languages and most hearing-impaired children learn how to understand these signals.

FRIENDS TOGETHER

SENSES COVERED
Sight.

LEARNING OPPORTUNITY
● To learn a little about how to communicate without using speech.

YOU WILL NEED
No special requirements.

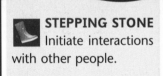

STEPPING STONE
Initiate interactions with other people.

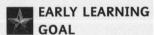

EARLY LEARNING GOAL
Personal, social and emotional development: Have a developing awareness of their own needs, views and feelings and be sensitive to the needs, views and feelings of others.

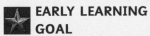

FRIENDS TOGETHER

SENSES COVERED
Sight.

LEARNING OPPORTUNITY
● To learn how to speak slowly and clearly so that others can lip-read.

YOU WILL NEED
No special requirements.

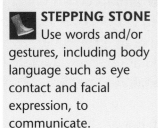

STEPPING STONE
Use words and/or gestures, including body language such as eye contact and facial expression, to communicate.

EARLY LEARNING GOAL
Communication, language and literacy:
Interact with others, negotiating plans and activities and taking turns in conversation.

Learning to lip-read

Sharing the game
● Explain that some hearing-impaired children learn how to lip-read, 'reading' the shape of words, rather than hearing the sounds of them.

● In order for them to do this, the words must be spoken very clearly.
● Ask your child to pretend that he cannot hear you and to attempt to lip-read what you are saying to him.
● Say that you will then reverse roles and see if you can lip-read what he is saying to you.
● Start by looking your child straight in the eye and mouthing a very simple sentence, which involves your child performing an action of some kind, for example, 'Please sit down'.
● You will know if he has understood you by the action he takes.
● Gradually increase the complexity of what you are mouthing and see if your child can continue to understand you. Use appropriate facial expressions to help him.
● Now reverse roles and invite your child to attempt to make you understand him by mouthing sentences to you.
● At first, it is likely that he will not mouth words very clearly or will whisper them.
● Explain that he must not speak at all, even very quietly.
● It will be easier for you to understand him if he over-emphasises the movement of his mouth as he attempts each word.

Taking it further
● Suggest that he looks in a mirror as he mouths words to see whether he can understand himself.

FRIENDS TOGETHER

FRIENDS TOGETHER

SENSES COVERED
Hearing, sight.

LEARNING OPPORTUNITY
● To use different senses to learn about an object, without using the sense of touch.

YOU WILL NEED
A number of fabrics of different textures.

 STEPPING STONE
Show an interest in what they see, hear, touch and feel.

 EARLY LEARNING GOAL
Creative development: Respond in a variety of ways to what they see, hear, touch and feel.

No feeling

Sharing the game
● Discuss what it means to have difficulty experiencing the different feel of things.
● Can your child suggest any ways that she could help a friend with these difficulties?
● Encourage her to think how the other senses of hearing and sight could help.
● Ask your child to imagine that she is unable to feel the texture of things. She has to guess what the fabrics will feel like just by looking very carefully at them.
● When she has had a good look, ask her to describe the texture of one or two fabrics to you, using words such as rough, smooth, furry, velvety, thick, thin and so on.
● Now encourage your child to feel the chosen fabrics and to describe the texture as she does so.
● Do these descriptions match her previous ones, when she was describing the fabrics by look alone?
● Point out how accurate (or inaccurate!) her visual descriptions were.
● If they were very inaccurate, help her to look more closely to discover much more detail.
● Would listening to your child's verbal descriptions help you to imagine what the fabrics felt like, if you were unable to touch them?

Taking it further
● Can your child think of ways to describe the feel of water, grass, sand and other natural textures?

SENSES COVERED
Touch.

LEARNING OPPORTUNITY
● To understand how important an accurate sense of touch is in enabling one to perform fiddly tasks.

YOU WILL NEED
A thick pair of child-sized gloves; child's jacket with a zip; children's shoes with buckles and ones with Velcro fastenings; blindfold.

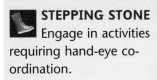

STEPPING STONE
Engage in activities requiring hand-eye co-ordination.

EARLY LEARNING GOAL
Physical development: Handle tools, objects, construction and malleable materials safely with increasing control.

How frustrating!

Sharing the game
● Blindfold your child loosely or ask him to close his eyes.
● Start by inviting your child to do up his jacket zip, once you have started it off. Point out how his fingers feel for and grip the slider in order to control it up or down.
● Put on his gloves and ask him to try again.
● Does this make the task harder?
● Explain that when his fingers are inside the thick gloves, his sense of feeling is very much diminished. This makes it extremely hard for him to locate and manipulate things, and to perform fiddly actions, especially when he cannot see.

● Now move on to the shoes. Without gloves, your child will probably be able to put on his shoes and cope with Velcro fastenings simply by feel, and he may be able to attempt slipping the strap through the buckle, even if he can't actually do the shoe up.
● With gloves on, the whole task becomes much more difficult. Your child has to find the right way to put the shoe on, locate the fastenings and then manipulate them, all without seeing and with very restricted feeling in his fingers.

Taking it further
● Remove the blindfold.
● Ask your child to attempt cutting up a plate of his food while holding a knife and fork normally, and then with gloves on.
● Discuss the difference.

SENSES COVERED
Sight, hearing, smell.

LEARNING OPPORTUNITY
● To learn how to use the other senses when it is not possible to taste.

YOU WILL NEED
A day when your child has a cold and is finding it hard to identify different tastes.

 STEPPING STONE
Show some understanding that good practices with regard to eating can contribute to good health.

EARLY LEARNING GOAL
Physical development: Recognise the importance of keeping healthy and those things which contribute to this.

No taste

Sharing the game
● Explain the fact that sometimes our sense of taste is diminished when we have a cold.
● We have to rely on our senses of sight and hearing to help us to appreciate what it is we are eating, and to imagine the wonderful tastes we are missing out on.
● At lunchtime, put some favourite food in front of your child and let her confirm that she has very little sense of taste at the moment by trying a small mouthful.
● How could she make the eating of her meal more pleasurable?
● Suggest that she looks carefully at her meal to see the variety of colours and appetising look of her food. She will be able to see that she likes the food you are offering her. This should make her want to eat it, despite the fact that she cannot taste it that well.

● Hearing you encouraging her to eat by describing the favourite food you are offering, should also enable her to imagine the tastes.

Taking it further
● Ask your child to describe various pictures of plates of food found in food magazines. Encourage her to make each meal sound as appetising as possible, by describing colours, tastes, textures and smells, so that someone who has lost their sense of taste will want to eat them.

No smell

SENSES COVERED
Hearing.

LEARNING OPPORTUNITY
● To appreciate the importance of our sense of hearing when we cannot smell.

YOU WILL NEED
A sensitive smoke alarm on the wall; an old alarm to look at; toaster and some bread.

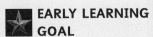 **THINK FIRST!**
Make sure your child realises that a toaster gets very hot and he must not touch it. Warn him of the loud noise the alarm will make.

STEPPING STONE
Further explore an experience using a range of senses.

EARLY LEARNING GOAL
Creative development: Respond in a variety of ways to what they hear.

Sharing the game
● Explain that our sense of smell is not always as good as we would like it to be.
● Sometimes we do not smell things that could be potentially dangerous to us.
● It is, therefore, very important to have an alarm that can send us a warning signal.
● Discuss situations where we need to be able to smell dangers, for example, smoke, gas leaking and so on.
● Talk to your child about smoke alarms and let him see what one looks like. Discuss their purpose.
● Let him see how one is set off and produces a warning signal.

● Set up the toaster close to the smoke alarm.
● Toast a piece of bread for long enough to burn it slightly and produce a small amount of smoke.
● If the alarm is sensitive enough, it should be set off, having picked up the 'smell of the smoke'.
● The loud noise it gives out warns us that we must do something to prevent a fire.
● In the case of the toast burning, what should we do?

Taking it further
● Discuss other warning signals (for example, food giving us a horrible taste in our mouths if we have failed to notice that the food is off and smelling bad).

SENSES COVERED
Sight.

LEARNING OPPORTUNITY
● To introduce sensory provisions into small-world play.

YOU WILL NEED
A set of play-people with their cars, trains and houses; A3 card; black, green, red and yellow thick felt-tipped pens; scissors; bubble wrap; modelling clay; masking tape; straws.

 STEPPING STONE
Use one-handed tools and equipment.

 EARLY LEARNING GOAL
Physical development: Handle tools, objects, construction and malleable materials safely and with increasing control.

Help outside

Sharing the game
● As you go out and about, look for safety features outside provided for those with sensory disabilities. For those who cannot see, there are bumpy surfaces to feel at the edge of pavements and at pedestrian crossings, and a bleeping sound at pelican crossings; for those who cannot hear, there are green and red men at pelican crossings and yellow lines at the edge of station platforms.
● Explain the purpose of each of these and how they particularly help those with sensory impairments.
● Invite your child to draw out a road on the card and outline a pavement using the felt-tipped pens.
● Let your child draw a green walking man and a red stationary man on to card. Help her to cut them out and tape them back to back on to a straw.
● Stick the straw into the modelling clay and place it between the road and the pavement.
● Next to this sign, let your child tape a small piece of bubble wrap, to indicate the bumpy surface at the end of the pavement.
● Encourage your child to use this play situation realistically with some of her small-world people who have sensory impairments.

Taking it further
● Draw train tracks on another piece of card and use two play bricks at the side of the track as a platform.
● Next, draw bright yellow lines at the edge of each platform to warn people who cannot hear trains approaching that they shouldn't stand too close to the edge.

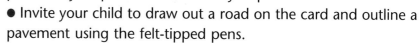

Encourage your child to be aware of his five senses – sight, hearing, touch, smell and taste. Invite him to use his imagination to the full, so that he can appreciate the delicious smells and tastes, the interesting sounds, the wonderful sights and the delightful feel of things described in the rhymes.

I love little pussy

I love little pussy, her coat is so warm,
And if I don't hurt her, she'll do me no harm.
So I'll not pull her tail, nor drive her away,
But pussy and I very gently will play.
I'll sit by the fire, and give her some food,
And pussy will love me because I am good.

Traditional

USING THE RHYME
If you have a cat, invite your child to stroke her pet as you say the rhyme together. Encourage her to listen out for purring. Alternatively, invite her to stroke one of her soft toys. Emphasise the need for gentleness when handling small animals. See the game 'Snug as a bug!' on page 12.

Pease porridge hot

Pease porridge hot,
Pease porridge cold,
Pease porridge in the pot,
Nine days old.

Some like it hot,
Some like it cold,
Some like it in the pot,
Nine days old.

Traditional

It's raining, it's pouring

It's raining, it's pouring,
The old man is snoring,
He went to bed and bumped his head,
And couldn't get up in the morning.

Traditional

USING THE RHYME
When it is raining hard outside, say the rhyme together. Listen out for thunder, look for lightning, listen to the noise of the rain on the roof and notice the raindrops running down the window pane. When the rain eases off a little, go outside and feel the raindrops landing gently on your hands and face. See the game 'What shall I wear?' on page 15.

USING THE RHYME
Say the rhyme together. Has your child ever tasted porridge? How would he like his? Try making some porridge with your child. Notice how the texture changes when the hot porridge has gone cold. See the game 'Hot or cold?' on page 26.

100 OUR SENSES

Jack Sprat

Jack Sprat could eat no fat,
His wife could eat no lean,
And so between them both,
They licked the platter clean.

Jack ate all the lean,
Joan ate all the fat,
The bone they picked clean,
Then gave it to the cat.

Traditional

USING THE RHYME
Explain the difference between fat and lean meat, by looking at streaky bacon, pork or lamb chops. Say the rhyme together and discuss whether Jack's wife was having a healthy diet by eating all that fat. Discuss table manners! See the game 'What can I taste?' on page 28.

The Queen of Hearts

The Queen of Hearts
She made some tarts,
All on a summer's day.
The Knave of Hearts
He stole the tarts,
And took them clean away.

The King of Hearts
Called for the tarts,
And beat the knave full sore.
The Knave of Hearts
Brought back the tarts,
And vowed he'd steal no more.

Traditional

USING THE RHYME
See the game 'The Queen of Hearts' on page 44.

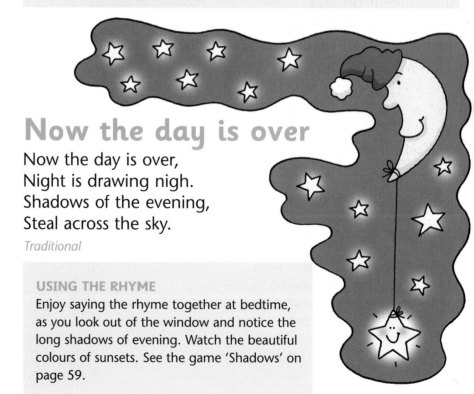

Now the day is over

Now the day is over,
Night is drawing nigh.
Shadows of the evening,
Steal across the sky.

Traditional

USING THE RHYME
Enjoy saying the rhyme together at bedtime, as you look out of the window and notice the long shadows of evening. Watch the beautiful colours of sunsets. See the game 'Shadows' on page 59.

100 OUR SENSES

Polly put the kettle on

Polly put the kettle on,
Polly put the kettle on,
Polly put the kettle on,
We'll all have tea.

Sukey take it off again,
Sukey take it off again,
Sukey take it off again,
They've all gone away.

Blow the fire and make the toast,
Put the muffins down to roast,
Blow the fire and make the toast,
We'll all have tea.

Traditional

USING THE RHYME
Under careful supervision, show your child how to make a cup of tea. Do the appropriate actions together while reciting the rhyme, substituting Mummy for 'Polly' and your child's name for 'Sukey' as you do so. Make some toast or toasted muffins to go with your tea. See the game 'Bathtime songs' on page 77.

My eyes can see

My eyes can see.
(make spectacles with hands)
My mouth can talk.
(bring index finger down on thumb repeatedly)
My tongue can taste.
(stick out and waggle tongue)
My ears can hear.
(cup hand and put behind ear)
My feet can walk.
(palms down, wriggle second and third fingers)
My nose can smell.
(touch nose with fingertip)
My teeth can bite.
(palms together, move fingertips together and back)
My eyelids can flutter.
(hold hands close to eyes, move fingers up and down)
My hands can write.
(pretend to hold pencil and write)
My fingers can feel.
(drum fingertips on the table)

Anonymous

USING THE RHYME
Emphasise all of the different senses and encourage your child to join in with the actions as you say the rhyme together. See the game 'What are my senses?' on page 85.

Summer breeze

Summer breeze, so softly
blowing,
In my garden pinks are
growing.
If you go and send the
showers,
You may come and smell
my flowers.

Traditional

USING THE RHYME
Say the rhyme together and
encourage your child to
imagine being in a garden
with the wind gently blowing
before the rain comes. If
possible, take her outside into
a garden after a spell of heavy
rain and let her smell the very
strong smell of the flowers.
Show her what pinks look like.
See the game 'Smell and
touch to "see" ' on page 115.

Six raisin-pear cakes in the baker's shop

Six raisin-pear cakes in the baker's shop,
Round and golden with a cherry on the top.
Along came _____ with a penny one day,
Bought a raisin-pear cake and took it away.

Five raisin-pear cakes…

Adapted from the traditional rhyme 'Five Currant Buns'

USING THE RHYME
Give your child a handful of pennies. Say the rhyme together using your
child's name and invite him to buy the cakes, one by one, using the
pennies. Encourage him to guess how many are left before checking the
number, as he takes each one away. See the 'The bakery' on page 105.

This is the way the ladies ride

This is the way the ladies ride,
Nimble, nimble, nimble, nimble.
This is the way the gentlemen ride,
A gallop, a trot, a gallop, a trot.
This is the way the farmers ride,
Jiggety-jog, jiggety-jog.
And when they come to a hedge – they jump over!
And when they come to a slippery space –
They scramble, scramble, scramble,
Tumble-down Dick!

Traditional

USING THE RHYME
Say the rhyme together with your child sitting on your lap. Start off gently
to imitate riding slowly. As the riding becomes faster and faster, make the
movements more energetic, lifting up both yourself and your child as they
jump over the hedge. Finish with your child 'falling' down between your
legs as Dick tumbles off. See the game 'Let's get fit!' on page 110.